BON APPÉTIT PARIS

MARA GRIMM

BON APPÉTIT PARIS

A GUIDE TO EATING AND LIVING IN EUROPE'S MOST STYLISH CITY

PRESTEL
Munich · London · New York

CONTENTS

PREFACE   7

1. LE BON GOÛT
The importance of taste   12
Je suis snob   15
Name dropping   18
Unfaded glory   22
The Parisian diet   24

2. LE PETIT DÉJEUNER
The best baguette in Paris   28
Croissants with extra butter   38
Le pain au chocolat   48
French breakfast   52
Sock-water coffee   56

3. LE DÉJEUNER
Holy lunch   62
My favourite lunch dish   68
Un steak, s'il vous plaît   74
The prince of Paris   80
Mouth-watering omelettes   84
Crêpes & galettes   90
Cursing in the Sacre-Cœur   92
La vie en beurre   94

4. LE GOÛTER

Cakes and champagne	104
Macarons	108
Of old masters and Instagram stars	112
Puffs of happiness	118
Le thé	124
The art of chocolate	126
Glace parisienne	132

5. L'APÉRO

The French wine lobby	138
Prendre un verre	142
Champagne tous les jours	148
Le pique-nique	156

6. LE DÎNER

44,000 restaurants	162
Le bistro	166
La brasserie	176
Fruits de mer	184
Le bouillon	188
Old and new stars	194
La cave à manger	202
The new Paris	206

7. PARIS À LA MAISON

Cooking constitutes buying	212
Tableware addict	222
The etiquette of groceries	228
Haute légume	231
Gastronomy from the freezer	234
1200 cheeses	236
Tout caramel	246

À BIENTÔT	248
LES ADRESSES	250

PREFACE

For as long as I can remember, I knew that one day I would go and live in Paris. I would dream of the cliché: sitting in cafés and writing, contemplating the zinc roofs, going to the bakery each morning for a fresh baguette, enjoying a glass of wine at lunch and walking the streets for hours on end. My dream came from actually seeing this life lived: from the moment I started walking, my mother would take me with her to Paris twice a year to be immersed in art, gastronomy, fashion, beauty and life. We would browse the main museums, have lunch in newly established bistros and enjoy meals in old brasseries. Paris was where I learned all the important lessons about love and life, in addition to less important ones about fashion and style.

I became fascinated with Parisians: their love of food, their penchant for beauty, their sense of quality and the great and mysterious *je ne sais quoi*, about which volumes have been written. Needless to say I have devoured the style guides by icons such as Inès de La Fressange and Caroline de Maigret.

When my dream came true seven years ago and I was able to move to Paris for some of the year, I was under the illusion that I knew exactly how Parisians live. But I was still missing something. Although thousands of lessons about the fashion, love and style of Paris have been written, what about the city's eating habits? Why do Parisians go out for lunch so often, and what is the best way to treat French waiters? What tableware is a must-have and why is it that food trends hardly ever catch on in Paris? And also important: what to wear when going to a restaurant? I decided to do some research. The result is this culinary style guide, the book I would have loved to have had when I was dreaming about a life in Paris.

1

LE BON GOÛT

If you want to eat like a Parisian, you need to become a snob immediately. But take note: it's all about quality, not expense.

THE IMPORTANCE OF TASTE

*P**ut six people at the table and the ritual commences: you open a bottle of champagne and discuss what you are going to eat. You continue by discussing what you are eating, followed by talking about what you have just eaten. And you conclude with a discussion about what you will be eating next week.*

This is how Alain Ducasse described the perfect Parisian evening in *The New York Times*. And he was not exaggerating. To Parisians, food is more than just nutrition; it is culture, desire, love – and sometimes even poetry.

In some cases, the love Parisians have for food is so extreme that the president is judged based on his culinary preferences. The fact that Mitterand was unfaithful to his wife was of no importance whatsoever, because that was *la vie privée*. Also, this president enjoyed the admiration of many due to his insatiable appetite. On his deathbed, he ordered ortolans, oysters, *foie gras* and capon. The French had more issues with Sarkozy. Nobody cared about the stories of his corrupt behaviour, but his decision to remove cheese platters from the Elysée Palace menu because he wanted to lose weight was utterly unforgiveable. This just goes to show that while you can get away with almost anything in France, you'll never get away with having bad taste.

JE SUIS SNOB

Liberté Egalité Snobiété

I put up a card in my kitchen: *Liberté, Egalité, Snobiété*. If you want to eat like a regular Parisian, you need to become a snob immediately. It is considered *bon ton* to tut-tut in disapproval for all that is mediocre. And it's always about quality, never about conspicuous consumption: a Parisian snob prefers a high-quality 1-euro baguette over a 50-euro can of mediocre caviar any time. Prices are of no importance whatsoever; it's having the crème de la crème that counts.

Parisians love contests, in the culinary areas in particular. They hold all kinds of hugely serious competitions, from the best bread in Paris to the best *oeuf mayo*, the tastiest éclair, the cow that provides the best meat and the very best *saucisse purée*. The list goes on and on. Parisians also love to decide what is best and are born judges. Snobby? *Mais non. Je ne suis pas snob, je suis Parisien.*

A CRASH COURSE IN CULINARY SNOBBERY

- Forget about supermarkets. Find a market or specialist shop for your grocery shopping. After seven years in Paris, for me it's perfectly normal to buy my cabbage lettuce at stand A, my chicory at stand B and my radishes two streets away.

- Choose the best quality you can afford. Better to eat a macaron from that great pastry chef once a week than a few cookies from the supermarket every day.

- Buy selectively. If the baker gives you a baguette that does not look quite crisp enough, nobody will frown if you ask for one that is *bien cuite*.

- In a best-case scenario, a real snob is only moderately enthusiastic. In Paris, you seldom hear someone saying that a dish was magnifique; usually, it's *pas mal*.

- Was that sauce a tad too salty? Your cake just that little bit too sweet? Chocolate mousse not airy enough, or the wine not what you expected? A snob will leave it – this also explains why most Parisians are so lean.

NAME DROPPING

For years now, Parisian style icons have been saying that wearing logos on clothing is a serious faux pas. A Parisian would rather die than be caught in the streets looking like a walking advertising board. My good friend Robin – a true-*bleu* snob from the Rue de Paradis – blatantly refuses to wear a t-shirt with even the smallest logo. He will take a key to scratch the logo off his Ray Ban's and even turns plastic bags inside out so nobody can see where they come from.

This may sound a bit extreme, but you will hardly ever see anyone in Paris wearing a t-shirt or sweater with the logo of a large fashion house. Chanel, Céline and Saint Laurent do make items with large logos, but these are almost exclusively sold to tourists. Parisians go by the basic assumption that you can buy your clothes wherever you want, but you never display designer names.

Name dropping is another *faux pas* in Paris. There is just one exception to this rule: when it comes to food. Food name-dropping is perfectly okay and it's more than *bon ton* to flaunt the names of producers and suppliers. Menus commonly state them and some restaurants even put the names of their suppliers in large letters on their windows: *Ici nous vendons des glaces Berthillon!* So there is not a Parisian soul who needs or wants to know that your bag is Hermès, but if your truffles are from Galis, your radishes from Erwan Humbert, courgettes from Domaine de Vernins or asparagus from Robert Blanc, you can shout it from the rooftops as loud as you like.

SEVEN NAMES TO IDOLISE

Alain Milliat
Twenty five years ago, farmer's son Alain shipped his fruit juices to the best sommeliers in France. And they were a hit: today, Milliat is a key component of Parisian menus. His tomato juice is especially delicious.

Jean-Yves Bordier
There is simply no way escaping Jean-Yves Bordier's butter: his name is spelled in giant letters on all of the menus, no exceptions.

Le Prince de Paris
Branded with the Eiffel Tower and lovingly referred to as Le Prince de Paris, this is the only ham that is still produced in Paris. Celebrated by top chefs such as Yannick Alléno.

Pierre Hermé
The ultimate Lord of the Macaron and godfather of the new generation of pastry chefs. If you come across his cakes anywhere, be sure to order them!

Poilâne
Although you might associate France with baguettes, sourdough bread is actually more traditional. The Poilâne family has kept this great tradition for no fewer than three generations. Baked in wood-fired ovens, Poilâne bread is made from four ingredients: flour, water, salt from Brittany and a sourdough starter.

Alain Ducasse
Alain Ducasse is a top chef who owns several starred restaurants in addition to a chocolate empire. In just a few years, his chocolate has become the best in the city.

Champignons de Paris
There was a time when extensive mushroom cultivation took place under the streets of Paris. In the nineteenth century, the city featured over three hundred mushroom growers; today, few are left. So if you ever come across real Champignons de Paris on a menu, be sure to order them.

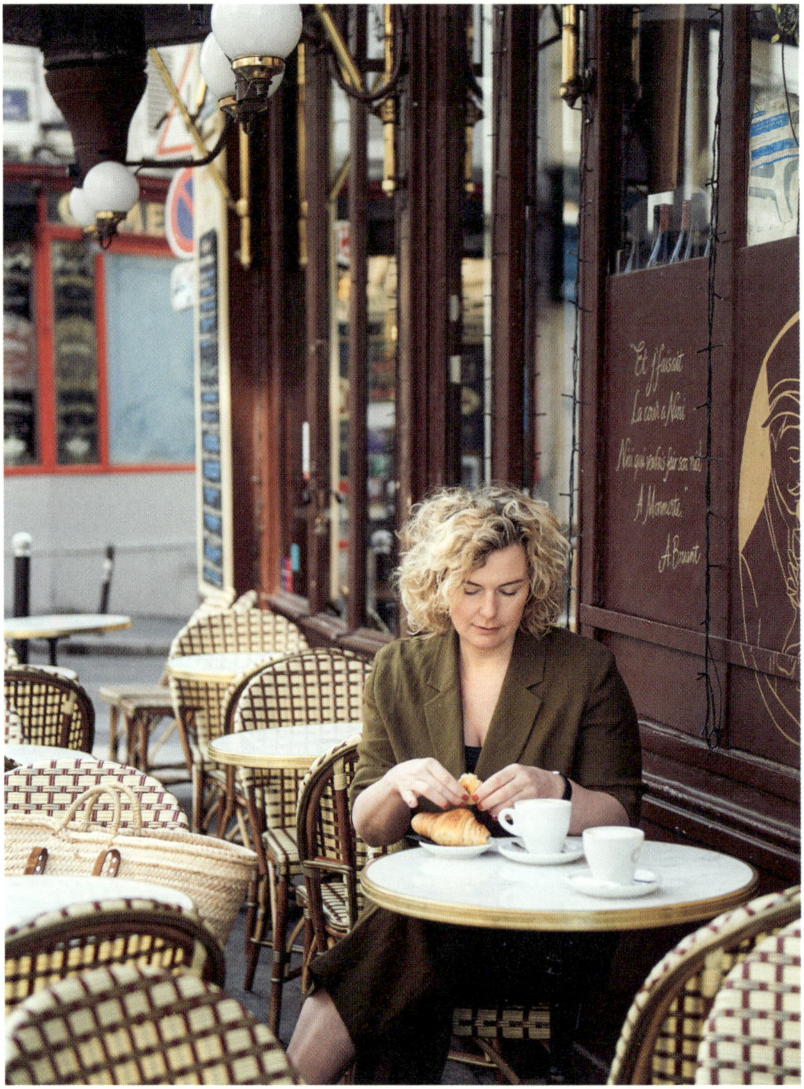
Et j'faisait
La cour a Nini
A Bruant

UNFADED GLORY

Even after seven years in Paris, I never get tired of seeing those Parisians who seemingly casually threw on the right blouse, perfect sweater or somewhat oversized jacket. I am aware now that this casualness is merely appearance; their cavalier and elegant look is carefully supplemented with heirlooms, vintage bracelets and cashmere sweaters. Trends hardly ever have anything to do with this. After all, it's all about the classics.

This approach is also part of Paris gastronomy. Similar to the Parisian wardrobe, Parisian cuisine is averse to trends. Food trends hardly ever catch on in Paris, while classics are revered. Just as an outfit should have a certain degree of casualness, dishes should not look too neat or well-considered. Flowers and complicated garnishing? *Mais non!* Similar to Parisian women who will wear no more than one piece of jewellery, Parisian chefs will limit themselves to main ingredients, but they must excel in quality and simplicity. There's no such thing as too basic. Too old school? Not at all. After all, why innovate if the best has already been invented?

French gastronomic culture is maintained at all costs. If a dish runs even the smallest risk of passing into oblivion, immediate action is taken. Camembert made from pasteurised milk? *Mais non*, this should be forbidden!

I saw the best example of this during the lockdown. Paris felt quieter than ever, but nothing seemed to change in the delicatessens. The selection at La Grande Épicerie at the Rue de Sèvres seemed even more spectacular than before: every day, oysters, lobsters and crabs were showcased as if it were Christmas time. There were *foie gras*, cans of caviar and various cheeses. And although there weren't many customers around, the manager walked around in a three-piece suit dusting the bottles of wine with a feather duster. The message was clear: schools and restaurants may be forced to close, parties forbidden and curfews imposed, but nothing and nobody interferes with Parisian food – not even a pandemic.

This compulsive preservation of their gastronomic culture has a reassuring – or even romantic – touch. But it also means that any innovation in Paris is approached with the necessary scepticism. This has been the case since the distant past. When, in around 1884, the plans for the construction of the Eiffel Tower were published, the entire city was in a state of uproar, and once erected, people wanted it to be dismantled immediately. The same goes for new restaurants. In any other metropolis, a new venue would be fully booked the very first week, but not in Paris. Here, residents turn a blind eye instead.

So, instead of embracing anything new, Parisians cling to the status quo. One obvious consequence is that menus in brasseries and classic bistros hardly ever change. There have been developments, certainly, such as the introduction of the bistronomy and the fusion of French and Japanese cuisine. This, however, does not alter the fact that Parisians still worship venues such as Café de Flore, Bofinger and La Coupole. If an iconic bistro is on the verge of bankruptcy, someone will come to the rescue. Faded glory? There's no such thing in Paris. Everything is perfectly maintained, paint touched up and every speck of dirt polished off. Paris remains a city of unfaded glory.

THE PARISIAN DIET

Writing about diets is something of a taboo for me. After all, the task of the culinary journalist is to promote the good life. But let me say something about it anyway, because after my initial months in Paris, I lost the plot for a bit. I immensely enjoyed my daily breakfast of croissants, going out for lunch every afternoon and the various glasses of wine every evening, complemented by a few cigarettes. But after two months I was worn out by all those copious meals, litres of wine and long evenings. How on earth do Parisians keep this up in a city heaving with restaurants, cafés and chocolatiers?

The answer is simple: moderation. This sounds terribly boring, but the opposite is true. If it is normal for you to have a glass of wine with lunch on a regular basis, you won't want to go boozing during the weekend as much. If you go out for lunch every day, two courses will do. And if you are not too particular about a little fat on your meat, you are not so inclined to wolf down that bag of crisps. So if you do not have to contain yourself all the time, you are less inclined to overdo it.

I'll never forget my friend Willemiek's surprise when she stayed with colleagues in Paris. In the morning when croissants were served, she took one and ate it. Her French colleagues took one and shared it among the three of them.

This shows how Parisians deal with food. Nobody fusses about butter, wine or madeleines. In Paris, it is best not to be bothered about rich or greasy food, because this is what gives food its flavour. Or, as the French say: *Le gras c'est le goût, le goût c'est le gras* (Fat is flavour, flavour is fat). This by no means alters the fact that moderation is key and snacks are avoided. You will seldom see anyone eat or drink in public, there was even a time when this was prohibited in Paris. Most Parisians exclusively eat at five fixed times, all with their own rituals and traditions. I'll discuss these in the following chapters.

Le petit-déjeuner	*Breakfast*	08.00–10.00 am
Le déjeuner	*Lunch*	12.00–14.00 pm
Le goûter	*Something sweet*	16.00–16.30 pm
L'apéro	*The aperitif*	18.00–20.00 pm
Le dîner	*Dinner*	20.30–23.00 pm

2

LE PETIT-DÉJEUNER

Hold onto your buttery
croissants: the classic
French breakfast has little
to do with food.

Never consider buying a house in Paris in a district without a good bakery. This was the strong recommendation from a Parisian friend when I first went house-hunting in the French capital. The number of square metres, hot and cold water, a balcony or not... all of these details pale into insignificance when compared to having the best boulangerie in the arrondissement just around the corner. So my first apartment at 12 Rue Bochart de Saron was tiny, extremely noisy, cost me an arm and a leg and was extremely cold. There was no central heating and the wind blew harder inside than it did outside. I had to pay one year's rent in advance and would have to pay another small fortune for each nail I'd drive into a wall. But none of this ever bothered me, because it was near the Rue des Martyrs, which featured at least ten good bakeries and patisseries.

The French take their bread very seriously, which is obvious everywhere you look. It's even the talk of the day at my hairdresser's. During the months of the harvest, ears of wheat are given to regulars as the ultimate symbol for happiness, health and financial prosperity – which by the way is vital if you have a Parisian hairdresser. Even the language is interspersed with expressions using the word bread. For instance, a tedious event is referred to as *long comme un jour sans pain* (long as a day without bread).

In Paris, the baguette is an essential part of daily life. So much so that a contest is held each year to decide who bakes the best baguette in the city: the prestigious concours du *Grand Prix de la baguette de tradition Française de la ville de Paris*. Each participating bakery submits two baguettes. Some competitors drop out immediately because they fail to comply with basic baguette requirements: the loaves must measure between 55 and 65 cm long and weigh 250 to 300 grams. Baguettes that make it to the next round are allocated a number so the jury can conduct a blind test. The jury – consisting of chefs, journalists and retired bakers – evaluate *cuisson*, texture, aroma and taste. Baguettes must have a slightly sweet taste and an aroma with a hint of apricot. They must have a thick and crisp crust that cracks when a small piece is broken off. The crumbs must be elastic, but definitely not rubbery, and must contain irregular air bubbles. Tough requirements indeed, but much is at stake here: the winner may provide the president of France with bread for a year and will gain many new customers. You can identify the winners by the sticker in their window, and even more so by the queue of customers in front of their premises.

That being said, the French have cut back on their bread intake. There was a time when 320 baguettes were sold every second, but figures have been dropping for years. The French have been buying their baguettes at the supermarket more and more often, leaving bakeries to struggle – in the countryside in particular. Baguettes sold through automatic bread distributors are becoming increasingly familiar because bakers can hardly survive. I remember how amused I was when I saw one those machines for the first time somewhere in Normandy, but of course it is really *un drame*. Once a baker closes up shop, a village loses not just its bread; it loses its very soul.

Fortunately, the opposite is happening in Paris, where a new generation of bakers has emerged who focus on high-quality sourdough bread and baguettes. Many of them have stickers reading I LOVE GLUTEN above the counter for their young and trendy customers to read before buying top-quality bread. The best of these entrants is without doubt Boulangerie Mamiche at the Rue Condorcet. Guess who I now live around the corner from.

♀ THREE FAVOURITES

La Parisienne The most recent winner of the award for the best baguette of Paris. *12, Rue du Faubourg-Poissonnière, 10th*
Mamiche This is where I buy my baguettes, as well as some of the best almond croissants in the city. *45 Rue Condorcet, 9th*
Ten Belles Sourdough bakery and coffee paradise combined. *7 Rue Bréguet, 11th*

TARTINE BEURRÉE

The ultimate Parisian breakfast consists of nothing more than a crisp baguette with a layer of butter thick enough to shock even me. Made with the best quality bread and butter ever, *une tartine beurrée* is the epitome of gastronomy, certainly when dipped in to your *café crème*. French author Colette famously stated: *Le vrai gourmet est celui qui se délecte d'une tartine de beurre comme d'un homard grillé.* Translation: real connoisseurs appreciate bread and butter as much as they appreciate a grilled lobster.

A CRASH COURSE IN BAGUETTES

- Bakeries provide two choices in baguettes: a *baguette tradition* or a *baguette classique*. The *tradition* is the better choice. It must be baked on location, free from any bread improvers. A *tradition* is recognised by its thin and pointy shape, crisp caramel crust and creamy white crumb.

- The *classique* or *ordinaire* is about ten cents less in price, but not as tasty. Its crust is paler and less crisp, with a mealier, drier crumb. Its shape is also different: *classique* ends are round instead of pointy.

- You won't need to use the word baguette when ordering at the baker; simply saying *une tradition, s'il vous plaît* will do.

- Feel free to ask for a well-done or medium baguette: *une baguette bien cuite* or *pas trop cuite*. I usually choose the first option because of the lovely crisp crust, but a softer crust is better for dipping in sauce during dinner.

- Baguettes become stale in a surprisingly short time, so it's perfectly normal to go to the bakery twice a day. If you don't need an entire baguette, simply ask for *une demie*. A baguette will last a little longer if you wrap it in a linen cloth. Tip: special cotton or linen bread bags are sold for storing baguettes.

- The French have a lovely tradition: they break off the end of the baguette on the way home and eat it. In the south, this end is called *le quignon*, in the north *le cul*. In Paris, it's referred to as *le croûton*.

CROISSANTS WITH EXTRA BUTTER

Shortly after I moved to Paris, one of the first things I did was set out on a quest for the best croissant in the city. Seven years have since passed, and still I haven't found it. Or, to be more precise: I find a new one every month. From the elongated croissants of the Ritz to the somewhat smaller ones by La Maison d'Isabelle: Paris has croissants of all types and sizes.

A good croissant is made from flour, yeast, sugar, salt, water and butter – heaps of butter. Some bakers make it their life's goal to put as much butter in a croissant as possible. Croissants with a butter content of 40 per cent are no exception. However, a croissant should never be dripping with grease. The inside should be airy, with a golden exterior. And the crust? It must be crisp and a little *flaky*. Eating a croissant will certainly leave you with crumbs on your chin, but it should never fall apart like an apple turnover.

The French distinguish between a *croissant ordinaire* and a *croissant au beurre*. The first is baked using margarine instead of butter. You will recognise an *ordinaire* by its appearance: it's crescent-shaped, while a croissant made with butter is straighter. And although the *croissant au beurre* is generally better, croissants made with margarine have one main advantage: they are firmer and thus more suitable for dipping in coffee, which many French gourmands love to do. This explains why croissants made with margarine still enjoy huge popularity.

NOT FRENCH

Croissants are not at all French in origin and there are many, many stories concerning their true provenance. The most famous is set in Vienna in 1683, the year the Battle of Vienna ended and which marked the downfall of the Ottoman Empire. According to this story, the croissant was invented as the symbol of the victory over the Ottomans: it has the shape of the moon on the Ottoman Empire flag, the precursor to the current Turkish flag. It's an interesting anecdote, but Vienna was home to croissant-shaped cakes long before that time. Also, their structure deviated from the croissants we know and love, because they looked more like today's *brioches*. Needless to say, they were not referred to as croissants, but instead *kipfels*.

The story continues with Marie Antoinette, the Austrian princess who in the second half of the eighteenth century came to France to marry King Louis XVI. She was forced to sever any relation she had with her family and devote herself to her new homeland. But she never gave up her love for *kipfel*. She even changed its name to croissant to have her favourite breakfast accepted in France. Well, the same applies here: however interesting, the story is quite improbable. Even though French chef François de la Varenne devised a recipe for *pâte feuillettée* (puff pastry) as early as in 1653, the first croissants were not introduced in Paris until the nineteenth century.

So the most probable story does not feature any war victories or princesses, but it does involve Austria. Around 1830, Austrian August Zang opened a Viennese bakery at the Richelieu in Paris: Boulangerie Viennoise. His selection included *kipfel*, but airier than the original Austrian version. Parisians were enraptured with this delicious pastry and gave the kipfel a more French-sounding name: the *croissant*, because of its crescent shape.

HOW TO EAT A CROISSANT

There is really just one correct way to eat a croissant: you break off parts and put them into your mouth. Cutting a croissant lengthways and spreading butter or anything else on it is simply not done. After all, it's not a roll. A croissant is preferably eaten pure, and because of its high butter content, there's really no need for extra butter. Purists also fiercely object to this, although others swear by putting cold butter on a lukewarm croissant. If you are one of these, put some butter from the communal dish on the rim of your plate, break off a piece from your croissant and butter it using your knife. Although there are ongoing debates about using butter, jam on a croissant is a serious faux pas, because it dominates the subtle sweetness of the croissant.

BRIOCHE BELLY

In addition to croissants, Parisians have another breakfast favourite: brioches. The glazed, soft and sweet rolls are loaded with eggs and butter, making them taste just so much more luxurious than ordinary bread. And while bakeries sell the best brioches, they are available anywhere. Most supermarkets even showcase an entire shelf filled with brioches. In France, each region has its own variant. The *brioche Parisienne* is a high and round roll. I like it with salted butter and some raspberry jam or honey. Did you know that the brioche have even enriched French language with the phrase *prendre de la brioche* – which translates into growing a belly. I won't comment on how fattening they are, but I do think a brioche belly does not sound half as bad as a beer belly.

That being said, brioche comes under the category of *viennoiserie*; a collective name for Viennese pastries, which include croissants, *pains au chocolat* and *pains aux raisins*. The term was invented by Austrian baker August Zang – the very person above who invented croissants and owned the Boulangerie Viennoise bakery. *Viennoiserie* is eaten in the morning and other pastries commonly in the afternoon for *goûter*.

FRESH

Parisians have a somewhat more extreme concept of fresh than most other people do: croissants should be eaten within four hours of coming out of the oven. However, older ones are often used for making almond croissants – one of the most delectable pastries ever.

ALMOND CROISSANTS

This recipe is a blend of the one by baker Éric Kayser and cookery book author David Lebovitz.

———————————————————————————— MAKES 4

4 one-day-old croissants
50 grams of flaked almonds
Icing sugar
FOR THE SUGAR SYRUP
100 ml of water
50 grams of granulated sugar
Splash of rum or kirsch

FOR THE FRANGIPANE
50 grams of butter
60 grams of ground almonds
5 grams of cornflour
50 grams of fine sugar
1 large egg
A few drops of almond extract
Salt

———————————— PREPARATION ————————————

Preheat the oven to 180 °C and line a baking tray with baking paper. Combine all of the ingredients for the frangipane in a bowl and mix for several minutes.

For the sugar syrup: combine the water and sugar in a saucepan and bring to the boil. Boil for about a minute, then remove from the heat and allow to cool down. Add the rum or kirsch.

Cut the croissants in half lengthways. Brush the bottom half with the sugar syrup. Cover it with some frangipane and then the top of the croissant. Brush the top with sugar syrup and cover with some frangipane.

Push flaked almonds into the frangipane topping and put them on the baking tray. Bake for 15-20 minutes. Sprinkle with some icing sugar.

EIGHT HIGH-QUALITY CROISSANTS IN PARIS

1. Good thinking: these elongated croissants by pastry chef François Perret are easy to both eat and dip in your coffee. Buy them around the corner from the Ritz, at the Comptoir. *38 Rue Cambon, 1st* **2.** Handy when you are travelling by Eurostar: Carton is diagonally opposite Gare du Nord and sells award-winning croissants. *6 Boulevard de Denain, 10th* **3.** Croissants by Tapisserie are flaky, crisp and delicious. *16 Avenue de la*

Motte-Picquet, 7th **4.** Cédric Grolet sells the prettiest and most frequently photographed croissants in the city. *35 Avenue de l'Opéra, 2nd* **5.** When buying croissants at Mamiche, be sure to try their almond croissants. *45 Rue Condorcet, 9th* **6.** Croissants by Gaudard feature that irresistible, elegant and sweet taste. *22 Rue des Martyrs, 9th* **7.** Union belongs to the new generation of boulangeries selling fine bread and, truth be told, perfect croissants. *2 Rue Bleue, 9th* **8.** I truly apologise, but the croissants by Maison d'Isabelle are so tasty that they ran out before I could photograph them. *47 Boulevard Saint-Germain, 5th*

LE PAIN AU CHOCOLAT

Parisians are constantly in a rush. Except when food is involved. Food makes the world stop turning and nobody will try to jump any queue for food. Missing *Le Metro*, even when another is coming in two minutes, constitutes sheer disaster for most Parisians, but standing in line at the butcher's because you are discussing the part of beef most suitable for a *pot-au-feu* for a quarter of an hour is not an issue. Indeed: discussing gastronomy seems to be a Parisian basic need.

The correct naming of chocolate croissants is an ongoing topic of discussion: should it be *chocolatine* or *pain au chocolat*? It is an issue that has been dividing France for years. President Emmanuel Macron's chef in the Élysée has even participated in the discussion. A fervent advocate of *pain au chocolat*, he will seize any opportunity to convince everyone in France that the word *chocolatine* is simply wrong.

People in the south-western part of France are great supporters of the word *chocolatine*. In Toulouse, some bakeries will charge 50 cents more if someone asks for a *pain au chocolat* instead of a *chocolatine*. Seven years ago, pupils of a local school submitted an official request to add *chocolatine* to French dictionaries – unsuccessfully, I might add. Nonetheless, a group of parliamentarians of the centre-right opposition party Les Républicains also attempted to include provisions in agricultural and food legislation that *chocolatine* was the one and only correct name. Alas, another proposition rejected.

To end the discussions and arguments for once and for all, a few years ago the bakeries interest group *La Fédération des Entreprises de Boulangerie* held an opinion poll, the results of which were as follows: 84 per cent of the French population prefers *pain au chocolat* and a mere 16 per cent chose *chocolatine* as their favourite term. End of discussion you'd think, right? Certainly; until the debate is rekindled – which never takes long in France.

♀ THREE FAVOURITES

Union This is where *pain au chocolat* is prepared with chocolate by Valrhona and divine butter. *2 Rue Bleue, 9th*

Cyril Lignac This boulangerie prepares *pains au chocolat* using top-notch butter from Poitou-Charentes. *133 Rue de Sèvres, 6th*

Boulangerie Malineau The perfect venue for a date: they sell double *pains au chocolat* – also a treat if you come alone. *3 Rue Vineuse, 16th*

PAIN AU CHOCOLAT BY JACQUEMUS

I think the very best *pain au chocolat* is literally a chocolate roll. I once had it at Café Citron, the restaurant that was once part of the Jacquemus fashion house. Now unfortunately closed, nevertheless this *pain au chocolat* is quick and easy to prepare. Buy a slim chocolate bar made from the finest dark chocolate you can find. Café Citron used the dark chocolate from À la Mère de Famille, the oldest sweet shop in Paris. You'll also need a baguette, preferably not too well done. Cut off a piece of baguette as long as the chocolate bar and cut it lengthways. Spread a generous amount of salted butter on both halves, put the chocolate bar between them, and it's ready. And don't you dare call it *chocolatine*.

FRENCH BREAKFAST

Hold onto your buttery croissants: the classic French breakfast has little to do with food. Their iconic breakfast of one cup of coffee and a cigarette originated in the first half of the nineteenth century. The French had been familiar with coffee for a long time and knew that coffee suppresses the sense of hunger. This is perfect for people who prefer not to spoil their appetite for extensive lunches and meals. Some would combine coffee with a piece of bread or sweet snack, but that would be it. From the time cigarettes were introduced around 1830, people ate even less for breakfast. Smoking suppressed that sense of hunger even more effectively than coffee. Hence the French breakfast became a sort of intermitted fasting *avant la lettre*. What today is the diet craze in the rest of the world, has characterised daily life in France for centuries.

Fast-forward two centuries, and this French breakfast is still as popular as it ever was. When I had just moved to Paris, I happily went along with this great morning ritual: a café crème and a few cigarettes at an outdoor café. Bringing a pen and paper was just for appearances; I was more preoccupied with watching other smokers passing by: mothers pushing a

pram, businessmen speaking loudly in their telephones, shop girls wearing perfect lipstick: they all had a cigarette dangling from their lips. And although I abandoned the habit years ago and today it's forbidden to smoke in many parks in Paris, I still eat very little breakfast. For the same reason people did two centuries ago: I don't want to spoil my appetite for lunch or a meal.

BRING YOUR OWN

So my recommendation when in Paris is to enjoy a light breakfast. Have breakfast at a café around the corner instead of your hotel. Cafés usually serve croissants from a nearby boulangerie. If they don't, buy one at the bakery to enjoy at the outdoor café; most cafés do not have any issue with this. Okay, so where to go? Parisians usually have their regular morning place nearby in their own *quartier*. Jane Birkin would occasionally eat a croissant at Les Arènes in the Rue Linné in the fifth. I like an outdoor café at the Avenue Trudaine. Their coffee is particularly terrible, but apparently I have spent so much time in Paris that this doesn't bother me anymore.

If you prefer an extensive breakfast, there are plenty of venues to choose from today. Locals mainly go for brunch, because that is some sort of lunch – and you know by now the importance of lunch to the French.

♀ THREE FAVOURITES

Tapisserie From the team at top restaurant Septime. Great croissants, even better coffee. *16 Avenue de la Motte Picquet, 7th*
Best Tofu This Chinese venue serves breakfast with velvety tofu pudding. *9 Boulevard de la Villette, 10th*
Hotel Amour When I didn't have my own place in Paris, I would often sleep here. I still come for the last orders or breakfast. *8 Rue de Navarin, 9th*

SOCK-WATER COFFEE

The greatest mystery of Paris is its coffee: to be precise, its embarrassingly inferior quality. After seven years, I still don't get why people who are perfectly okay with having to spend fifteen minutes in line at the neighbourhood's best pastry chef, discuss wine for hours on end and argue about the names of dishes, care so little about the quality of the coffee. Whenever you order a cup of coffee in Paris, it's likely that you will be served a cup of Richard, the French equivalent of Senseo. Watery, tasteless *jus de vaisselle* often served lukewarm. The French are not wrong when they refer to inferior coffee as *jus de chaussettes* or sock-water coffee. Despite attempts to improve this situation, they do not always succeed. One example is top chef Alain Ducasse, who set up various coffee bars in Paris a few years ago. They closed down very quickly due to insufficient *gusto*. However – and not before time – a new generation of baristas has emerged, increasing the number of addresses where you can enjoy a decent cup of coffee. There is one thing about this worth noting: these venues are commonly full of expats. It goes to show that most Parisians are still quite happy with their cup of sock water.

NO TO GO

Eating or drinking while on the go is just not done in Paris. I remember that, during my house-hunting days, I was oblivious to this and used to buy a coffee to go at KB on the Avenue Trudaine before visiting estate agents. I now know that Paris is not New York and nobody walks around drinking coffee. That is, except for me when I am looking for a house.

♥ MUST-HAVE: APILCO COFFEE CUPS

My dream to go and live in Paris one day was inextricably connected to coffee cups from Apilco, from one of the oldest porcelain factories in France. Bar du Marché in the Rue de Seine, which I frequented as a child, had them in a rainbow of colours. From the time I saw them, I fantasised about a kitchen filled with colourful porcelain. Meanwhile, Bar du Marché changed its crockery, as have most cafés and restaurants in Paris. After all, Apilco cups are costly and also rather impractical, because coffee tends to cool down in them very rapidly. Just be sure to preheat them thoroughly, which I do by filling them with boiling water. Yes, every morning – anything to live that dream. *www.apilco.com*

HOW TO ORDER COFFEE IN PARIS

- Some Parisian cafés charge three different prices for a cup of coffee: a *prix comptoir* for those who drink it at the bar, a *prix salle* when you drink it at a table and a *prix terrasse* when it is served to customers at the tables on the street. So you may be charged one single euro for a coffee at the bar and six times that amount for a *café crème* served outside. This explains the vivacity at French café bars early in the day.

- If you want a black coffee, order *un petit café*. Synonyms are *café express* or a *noir*; all of them names for an espresso. A *noisette* is the same, but with a splash of milk.

- An *allongé* is an americano, meaning that hot water is added to the coffee. Nice anecdote: this habit dates back to World War II, when American solders found French coffee to be too strong.

- Remember that in Paris a coffee with two thirds of warm milk is called a *café crème* and certainly not *café au lait* as many a tourist thinks. Although *café au lait* is served in France, they drink it in a large bowl with lots of milk. French people actually only have this for breakfast. When in a café, you order a *café crème*.

- Ordering a cappuccino in Paris is a bad idea, unless you are at a venue that specialises in coffee. For some obscure reason, cappuccino served in regular cafés is more expensive and does not taste nearly as good as a *café crème*.

3

LE DÉJEUNER

If you have ever wondered why Parisian restaurants are so busy at noon, you should know that in France it's actually forbidden to eat lunch at your desk.

HOLY LUNCH

In France, eating at your desk is legally prohibited. While this may sound like a dream or fantasy, Article R4228-19 of the Code du Travail actually reads: *Il est interdit de laisser les travailleurs prendre leur repas dans les locaux affectés au travail* (It is prohibited to allow workers to take their meals in areas assigned for work). Employers are thus obliged to provide proper lunches for their staff. If they do not have a canteen, they can choose to provide a lunch bonus or *tickets restos*; lunch vouchers that can be used to buy lunch at restaurants on working days. This is the most succinct explanation for the lively Parisian lunch culture. It also explains why small entrepreneurs still close shop from noon until 1.30 pm. Even the swimming pool around the corner from me closes its doors during lunch hours. At 11.30 am, the pool attendant calls out *Bon appétit Paris!* and everyone hurries out of the water to prepare for their midday meal.

I didn't realise just how important lunch is in Paris until the apartment of my dreams became available right beside the house I was living in. The timing was simply perfect: my tenancy agreement was soon to expire and I hadn't yet found a new place to live – although I had registered at dozens of estate agents. A few hours before viewing the apartment, I received a call from an acquaintance who said that if I had any real interest in that apartment, I had better get myself to the Rue du Bac to say a quick prayer. She was not kidding: some Parisians swear by a visit to the Chapelle Notre-Dame de la Médaille Miraculeuse (Our Lady Of The Miraculous Medal) at crucial moments in their life. So, an hour before the inspection, I cycled across the river Seine to Rue du Bac. You never know, right?

The chapel was closed. Naturally the nuns were having lunch and wouldn't be back before 2.00 pm… exactly at the time of my inspection. It goes to show that lunch really is sacrosanct in Paris. Sadly my dream apartment was sold to someone else from under my nose. I have no idea whether it had anything to do with that missed quick prayer, but my friend was convinced. I did know for sure that I would never ever again have lunch at my desk.

FORMULE DÉJEUNER

Going out for lunch takes far less time than you'd expect. Most bistros serve quickly so you're in and out in about three quarters of an hour. After all, lunches can't take too long, because people are expected back at work. If you have to be back at a certain time, you'd best order something from the daily menu, which is prepared more quickly and is less expensive compared to ordering à la carte.

People generally have a two-course lunch on workdays: a starter and a main course or a main course and dessert. In French: an *entree* + *plat* or a *plat* + *dessert*. These *formules déjeuner* come at a fixed price. Simple bistros charge about 19 to 25 euros for a two-course lunch – which immediately explains why they are packed with customers.

TABLE FOR ONE

I have a lot of friends who'd rather die than go out for a meal solo, but they are definitely not Parisians. In Paris, people are completely oblivious to this unease; a table for one is a perfectly normal occurrence, certainly during lunchtime. Many people enjoy lunch by themselves; from a widow ordering a dozen of oysters without batting an eyelid to a businessman tucking into a five-course lunch. No matter how diverse, solo eaters are without exception lovely people, because they are comfortable spending time by themselves and enjoy their food with total abandon.

After I moved to Paris, I mastered the art of eating alone at lightning speed. True, it happened initially out of necessity, because I only knew two people at first. Going to a restaurant by myself has long become voluntary and a true indulgence. Don't get me wrong: I love my friends, colleagues and family, but I simply concentrate much better on the flavours while watching service and listening to the customers' chatter. A *plat du jour*, a glass of wine and more than an hour to myself: sheer bliss.

SOLO EATING OUT FOR BEGINNERS

- Start by going out for lunch instead of dinner. In Paris, the chances that you are the only person eating alone are slim.

- Go to venues with lots of activity, such as a bistro with an outdoor café or a lively brasserie. You'll have plenty to see, which will make you feel less self-conscious than a tiny restaurant with candle-lit tables. Alternatively, go someplace you can eat at the bar.

- Don't start by ordering a five-course meal. Start out with one or two courses and increase the time you spend on your own in a restaurant from there.

- Don't hide behind your mobile phone, but instead look around; chances are you'll strike up a conversation with people at an adjacent table. Mind: the topic of these discussions will always be limited to food. After all, this is Paris.

- If you find it difficult to find something to do between courses, bring a book or writing pad and – my favourite pastime – imagine the life stories of the people around you.

- Never worry about people thinking you are sad or pathetic if you're sitting at a table by yourself. In Paris, eating solo is not confused with loneliness. In fact, if there is any place in the world where solitude is appreciated, this is it.

- Finally: do not hesitate to have a glass of wine during lunch but be sure to leave an establishment on the sober side. One glass will do.

MY FAVOURITE LUNCH DISH

As soon as a tradition is on the verge of disappearing into oblivion, all alarm bells in France will sound. In the 1980s when the classic bistro dish *œuf mayonnaise* – hard-boiled eggs and mayonnaise – was on the brink of being struck off Parisian menus, restaurant critic Claude Lebey jumped into action. For years on end, he had been using the following simple as well as affordable litmus test as the ultimate quality check for Parisian bistros. If it serves a good *œuf mayo*, you may assume the bistro is all right, because truth be told, the qualities of a chef will definitely be unveiled when preparing this dish. If the eggs are boiled too hard, poor-quality products are used or the garnish is substandard, you are immediately exposed. So, to prevent his favourite appetiser from becoming extinct, Lebey founded the *l'Association de Sauvegarde de l'Œuf Mayonnaise* (l'ASOM). Each year he would hold an extensive dinner at the restaurant where he had enjoyed the best *œuf mayo* that year.

Lebey died in 2017, but his grandson has put l'ASOM on the map again. The club even organises an annual World Championship for the best *œuf mayonnaise* on the planet. The jury for this contest consists of top chefs, prominent gastronomes and culinary journalists. Winners can expect a torrent of attention from the media and improved turnover for their restaurant. Bouillon Pigalle on the Boulevard de Clichy won the contest a few years ago. They used to sell one hundred and fifty *œufs mayo* per day, which increased to a stunning over four hundred following their win, so you could say Lebey's and his successor's plan was successful. Today, *œuf mayo* is the ultimate cult dish you will find on the menu of every self-respecting Parisian bistro.

INTEGRATION

During the second year that I lived in Paris, I became rather obsessed with this simple appetiser and I would order *œuf mayo* whenever I could. I was invited for an aperitif with Sébastien Mayol, chairman of l'ASOM, through a Parisian colleague of mine. After two bottles of wine and an hour's discussion about the perfect thickness of mayonnaise, Sébastien presented me with the best gift ever: my membership of l'ASOM. He said that this officially made me a Parisian. In short: my French was still disastrous, but I passed my integration course convincingly.

BREAKING THE RULES

The first and foremost point of attention for an *œuf mayo* is the egg: it must be fresh. I once spoke a chef who, on the day the World Championship was held, travelled ten hours by train to obtain the best fresh eggs in France. The egg yolk must be completely set but may definitely not be dry or crumbly. The same goes for the egg white: it must be set well but boiling it for too long will cause it to become rubbery. Finally: the mayonnaise. French mayonnaise is different to mayonnaise from other countries. In some countries, it is rather sweet, while the French type is pleasantly sour and a bit sharp with added mustard. But do note: if the mayonnaise used

for this dish is too sour, it may overpower the flavour of the egg. The garnish should never dominate: a slice of tomato, a few leaves of lettuce or a touch of grated truffle will do. Less is always more, which definitely applies to *œuf mayo*.

Then: presentation. The most beautiful *œuf mayo* I ever had in Paris was at Le Comptoir du Relais in the 6th arrondissement. Chef Yves Camdeborde arranges the eggs cut-sides down before coating them with a thin, even layer of mayonnaise. This can only be done with mayonnaise that is just that little bit thinner than it normally is, so usually it's diluted with some water. Accuracy is vital here: mayonnaise that's too thick won't form a nice coating, while watery mayonnaise will run off the eggs. If – like me – you lack the patience to coat the eggs with a sauce and are more a fan of thick mayonnaise, simply put the halved eggs yolk side up on a plate and use a piping bag to apply the mayonnaise. While it might not look quite as spectacular, the thicker mayonnaise could simply taste better than its diluted equivalent. The jury members of the World Championship seem to approve, given that former champion Bouillon Pigalle also uses a piping bag. It goes to show that rules are to be broken, even in Paris.

If you are looking for places where they serve a proper *œuf mayo* in Paris, fancy restaurants are not the place to go. The primary venues for this dish are the bistros and bouillons, where they usually cost just a few euros.

♀ THREE MORE FAVOURITES

Oui mon Général! High-end bistro owned by Stéphane Reynaud where delightful little eggs are served. *4 Rue du Général Bertrand, 7th*
Le Rubis This perfectly simple bistro serves perfectly simple *œufs mayo*; just the way they should be. *10 Rue du Marché Saint-Honoré, 1st*
Café des Ministères The place to be for a classic as delicious *œuf mayo*. *83 Rue de l'Université, 7th*

ŒUF MAYO BY PIGALLE

This recipe is based on that of Bouillon Pigalle, one-time winner of the World Championship. The quality of the eggs is crucial, so buy them at the market or from an organic farmer or farm shop instead of a supermarket. You only need to have two things to accompany your *œuf mayo*: a piece of baguette and a glass of wine.

———————————————————————— SERVES 2

2 large organic eggs
Coarse sea salt
Ice cubes
2 egg yolks
75 grams of Dijon mustard

500 ml of groundnut oil
4 grams of sherry vinegar
2 grams of salt
1 twist from the pepper mill
A handful of spinach leaves

———————————— PREPARATION ————————————

Put the eggs and some sea salt in a saucepan with cold water. Bring to the boil and allow them to boil for 9½ minutes. Transfer them into a bowl of iced water to stop the cooking process. Peel and halve the cooled eggs.

Meanwhile, prepare the mayonnaise. Put the egg yolks and mustard in a bowl and whisk together. Gradually add the oil and vinegar. Season with salt and pepper.

Fill a piping bag with mayonnaise. Arrange a few spinach leaves on a plate in a rosette. Use the piping bag to apply some dots of mayonnaise on the plate and put the eggs on top of them. Divide the rest of the mayonnaise between the flat sides of the eggs. Season with pepper as desired and serve.

UN STEAK, S'IL VOUS PLAÎT

The French are notorious omnivores. They actually always have been. When food shortages developed during the Franco-Prussian War, all six thousand horses of the Parisian taxi service were slaughtered and eaten. Dogs, cats, mice and rats faced the same fate. Eyes then shifted to the Jardin des Plantes zoo, but this proved somewhat more complicated. French butchers knew exactly how to slaughter horses, but an elephant? Apparently, the poor elephants Castor and Pollux underwent unnecessary suffering. Still, Parisians would go to incredible lengths to satisfy their appetite. The only creatures that were spared were the monkeys, lions and the hippopotamus; the monkeys resembled people too much, butchers were afraid to slaughter the lions and the hippopotamus was too expensive. No butcher was willing to pay big money for hippopotamus meat, because nobody knew if it was any good. If you are interested in more of these stories, be sure to get a copy of *A Bite-sized History of France*.

Even today, most Parisians eat whatever's going, from frog's legs to offal and rims of fat on the meat (yes, please!) to smelly andouillette. You really shouldn't be too fussy about food here. Although the number of places in Paris where they serve gluten-free bread and coffee with oat milk is increasing, French chefs are generally rather intolerant to intolerances.

So be sure to leave your dietary requirements at home and simply order a *steak frites*, for instance, still one of the most frequently ordered lunch dishes in Parisian establishments. It's on virtually every menu and comes in many variations and versions. My son and I have an ongoing competition to find the best in the city. From Au Bœuf Couronée in the nineteenth to the Le Relais De L'Entrecôte in the sixth: over the years we have checked off all the great classics. And although they themselves may think so, they are not by definition the best addresses.

AT THE BUTCHERS SHOP

So where to go for the perfect steak? While businessmen order it at La Bourse et La Vie in the 2nd arrondissement, the best meat in the city comes from its butchers. In Paris, some of them even have a few tables and chairs in their shop for their customers to eat on the spot. While you are eating, people from the neighbourhood come in to do some shopping and have a chat. This is where a low-key atmosphere is combined with top-quality. It makes sense, because who'd know better how to prepare meat than the butcher? One of the best eating experiences I ever had was at the premises of star butcher Hugo Desnoyer. He supplies many of the best restaurants in Paris, in addition to the Élysée Palace. Although he still has a butchers shop, customers can no longer eat there. Fortunately, other venues remain, such as The Butcher of Paris at the roofed Marché des Enfants Rouges, which I like best by far. Owner Louis-Marie Martin was once a wine merchant, so be sure to order a glass of natural wine with your steak.

SAIGNANT, S'IL VOUS PLAÎT

When ordering a steak, you'll be asked which *cuisson* you'd like: *bleu, saignant, à point* or *bien cuit*. Purists usually choose *bleu*, rare. I prefer *saignant*, which leaves the meat medium rare and deliciously juicy. *À point* refers to medium; also good but the meat may be somewhat drier. Never choose *bien cuit* (well done), because this is like eating the sole of a shoe.

♥ THREE FAVOURITES

The Butcher of Paris Wonderful location at the roofed Marché des Enfants Rouges. *38 Rue de Bretagne, 3rd*
Le Bon Georges The ultimate address for *steak tartare*. It is rather conservative, so don't get it into your head to order mayonnaise with your fries. *45 Rue Saint-Georges, 9th*
La Bourse et La Vie This is where you order the perfect *steak au poivre* served with chips fried using *blanc de boeuf*. *12 Rue Vivienne, 2nd*

THAT LOVELY PARISIAN ARROGANCE

Parisians have a penchant for complaining often and with conviction, in particular about their own city. They even sell t-shirts that read *J'aime rien, je suis Parisien*. On the other hand, there is the sacred belief that everything in Paris is better, be it fashion, art or food. There's no better place than the French capital for all of the above, and more. Or at least, so Parisians believe. Nobody has ever expressed this Parisian arrogance better than one of the first restaurant critics in Paris, Alexandre-Laurent Grimod de La Reynière: 'The best meat in the world may come from Poitou or the Auvergne, but it only tastes good when it is served in Paris.'

THE PRINCE OF PARIS

Let me prevent you from adopting too pretty a picture of French lunch culture: you can find plenty of Parisians who eat a roll at their desk, despite any act prohibiting them from doing so. *Le Parisien* or *le jambon-beurre* – consisting of a baguette, a staggering amount of butter and a few slices of cooked ham – plays an illustrious role here. In France, *Le Parisien* has an iconic status, with over three million of them sold every day.

If you have managed to find a good one, it's not merely a sandwich, but sheer bliss. But beware: that feeling of happiness can only come from all three ingredients being of superior quality. It's all about a crisp baguette, butter from the very best producers and the tastiest ham you can find. According to many Parisians, this can only be Le Prince de Paris. You can recognise this divine ham by the stamp of the Eiffel tower on it.

Le Prince de Paris is made by the last ham producer in the city at Rue de Charonne in the 11th arrondissement. They never really warmed to people looking over their shoulder, but at one time the owner Yves Le Geul invited me for a tour. It was an almost surreal experience to enter an old-school ham factory in the centre of Paris. Monsieur Le Geul swears by traditional methods and the flavours of the olden days, which is why everything here is done manually and only the best pigs from Brittany, Sarthe and Mayenne are selected. The hams are injected with a solution of Guérande sea salt before they are boned and brined. After nine hours of steaming, they are

stored in the refrigerator for eight days. This process leaves a pale pink ham with firm and juicy meat that tastes good enough to make Parisian top-restaurants swear by it… as do bakers and sandwich shops. The best-known of these may be Chez Aline, as evidenced by the queue at this former butcher shop where about five whole Prince de Paris hams are used every week.

♥ THREE FAVOURITES

Chez Aline In addition to le Prince de Paris, they also use butter by Maison Borniambuc here. *85 Rue de la Roquette, 11th*
Caractère de Cochon Although this small shop does not stock Prince de Paris, you can choose from all kinds of perfectly good hams. And since you are here: why not sample some of their excellent *choucroute*. *42 Rue Charlot, 3rd*
Le Petit Vendôme This old-school bistro serves extensive lunches with *œufs mayo* and *steak tartare*, in addition to quickly prepared *jambon-beurres*. *8 Rue des Capucines, 2nd*

RECIPE

JAMBON-BEURRE

Preparing your own *jambon-beurre* requires a good baguette – naturally the best you can find. Cut it lengthways but not all the way through and spread plenty of *beurre demi-sel* or *beurre salé* on both halves – the more, the better. I like the butter by Pascal Beillevaire with those salt crystals that crackle between your teeth. Then lay on about six slices of ham, preferably Le Prince de Paris, but any other high-quality cooked ham will also do. You could of course sprinkle on some thinly sliced cornichons, but then again: the purists will consider this sacrilegious.

MOUTH-WATERING OMELETTES

An omelette and a glass of wine is all you need for that perfect Parisian quick lunch. Not just any old omelette, of course, because preparing a good one is an art in itself. Some French chefs have young talents cook an omelette as part of their job application. If it complies with the set requirements, the interview is skipped and they are hired. Needless to say that if they fail, they can forget about the job. There's something magical about a perfect omelette that makes it difficult to believe it consists of nothing but eggs. In her book *An Omelette and a Glass of Wine*, English cookery writer Elizabeth David wrote about

Annette Poulard, owner of Hôtel de la Tête d'Or in Normandy. Her omelettes were so good that it left the entire French culinary scene buzzing and speculating about her secret ingredients. '*Foie gras*!' someone said. 'Cream!' another would yell. 'A special chicken breed?' the next asked. Finally someone asked Madame Poulard directly what her secret was in a letter. Her reply ended the discussion once and for all:

Monsieur Viel,

This is the recipe for the omelette: I break a few good eggs above a bowl, I beat them, put a generous lump of butter in a frying pan, add the eggs and continuously make circular movements with the frying pan. I am pleased, Sir, that you like this recipe.

Annette Poulard

In other words: once you know how to prepare a good omelette, you'll need few other ingredients. Above all, an omelette must be *baveuse* on the inside, that is: moist to the extent that you might wonder whether it's sufficiently done. I always considered *baveuse* a poetic word, until I learned that it is derived from *baver*, the French word for drooling. So an omelette should drool. However unsavoury the connotation of this word, it actually does convert an ordinary omelette into a small gastronomic miracle.

♀ THREE FAVOURITES

Pavyllon Not even the best of chefs turn up their noses at an omelette: I had one of the best ever in Yannick Alléno's breakfast bar. *8 Avenue Dutuit, 8th*

Omurice They're even a hit in usually trend-resistant Paris: the Japanese tornado omelette. *10, Rue de Port-Mahon, 2nd*

Au Sauvignon This is where omelettes with girolle mushrooms are prepared when in season. Very simple, extremely good. *80 Rue Saint-Pères, 7th*

À LA MAISON

If you are preparing an omelette at home, be sure it's *baveuse* and does not discolour while frying. It should be pale yellow without brown spots upon serving. It's important to take it from the frying pan in good time, because omelettes tend to keep cooking on the plate. Basic rule: it's better to remove it from the heat sooner than later. Then there is its shape; also of crucial importance. Make circular movements when frying so the omelette will move to one side of the pan to get an oval shape. Use a heavy frying pan without a non-stick coating. Try to avoid washing it and instead wipe it clean. I am not a supporter of kitchen gadgets and expensive apparatus, but I do have this special copper frying pan that is just perfect for omelettes. Finally: butter, and nothing but butter, is added to the frying pan.

OMELETTE NATURE

In Paris, menus usually come with all kinds of omelette fillings. I believe omelettes combined with cheese are highly overrated, so I usually choose the *omelette nature*. The one thing I add – in addition to a pinch of salt and pepper – is a lump of salted butter, which I put on my omelette right after removing it from the frying pan. Try this once and you'll never want it differently again.

PS: the French eat their eggs using a fork, meaning you don't divide an omelette in parts using a knife, but the side of your fork instead. Alternatively, use a piece of bread to put a piece of omelette on your fork.

— SERVES 1

2 eggs
A splash of cream

Salt and pepper
Butter

— PREPARATION —

Beat the eggs with the cream and add salt and pepper. Add a splash of water so the omelette becomes even moister.

Heat a lump of butter in a frying pan, allow it to sizzle out but do not let it colour. Add the eggs as soon as the sizzling stops and make circular movements with the frying pan.

Use a spatula to move the egg mixture to one side of the frying pan. Hold the pan at a 45-degree angle and tap the spatula against the side of the frying pan so the mixture will be oval-shaped.

Note: an omelette keeps cooking on the plate, so be sure to remove it from the pan sooner rather than later. Just let it slide onto a plate.

CRÊPES & GALETTES

The first time I walked along the Rue du Montparnasse was on my way back from a rather generous lunch at La Coupole. You should be aware that eating at a classic Parisian brasserie may involve huge amounts of bubbles – which I'll discuss later. Long story short: I had drunk so much that I thought I was suffering from double vision. I saw crêpes literally everywhere I looked. Turned out it wasn't the booze, but the Rue du Montparnasse, which resembles one big crêperie. Here's the thing: because the train from Brittany – where crêpes originated – historically arrived at Gare Montparnasse station, dozens of entrepreneurs opened crêperies there. From then on, crêpes conquered the entire city.

I honestly think the savoury buckwheat crêpes are better than their sweet equivalent. They are referred to as *galettes* and come in all kinds of versions, but the one with ham, cheese and an egg is unsurpassed. It's the perfect quick lunch, certainly when combined with a glass of Breton cider. Well, glass… cider should actually be served in a cup. For years, almost the entire culinary press was convinced that the ultimate address for cider was Breizh Café at the Rue Vieille-du-Temple. It became such a success that Breizh now has dozens of establishments frequented by masses of tourists. Too bad, but the advantage is that in Paris a Breizh Café is never far away. Luckily, they have successfully maintained their high standards. Their galettes are still served with traditional ham from Brittany, an organic fried egg, Comté cheese and – last but not least – a lump of butter by Bordier. *109 Rue Vieille-du-Temple, 3rd*

CURSING IN THE SACRÉ-CŒUR

The power of Parisian gastronomy is in retaining its traditions. Even the most pioneering French chefs still find themselves shackled by the traditions of French cuisine, making innovation rather a relative concept in this city. It may seem somewhat tedious to learn that most things have existed forever and will probably never change, but then again, the familiar also feels nice and safe.

Furthermore, every time I start wondering why it is that Parisian chefs make so few changes and variations to existing recipes, I am forced to face facts. I once found myself in a small establishment at the Canal Saint-Martin known for its different versions of *croque-monsieur*. I ordered one with hummus… on five-grain bread, no less. I took half a bite, just to see if it was really as bad as I thought it would be. It proved to be even worse. This was not just a simple tantamount in sacrilege; it was an utter tirade in the Sacré-Cœur. My craving for a classic *croque-monsieur* couldn't have been any greater than at that moment. Besides, there is already so much choice in classic *croques*. As for the bread: do you prefer *pain de mie* or sourdough? Crust on or off? Which ham do you choose? And, in the cheese department: Comté, Emmental or Gruyère?

I have since found my favourite version. I am too lazy to prepare my own béchamel sauce, so I use a generous amount of crème fraîche. Success guaranteed, provided you use a high-quality brand. I also use plenty of Dijon mustard. If you are not as addicted to a spicy flavour as I am, you could use a single teaspoon instead of two, but I think that all that fat could do with a fresh, tangy counterpart.

CROQUE-MONSIEUR

———— SERVES 1

50 ml of high-quality crème fraiche preferably from Isigny or Echiré
50 grams of Gruyère, grated
2 teaspoons of Dijon mustard

2 thick slices of white bread from a tin-loaf
1 slice of ham
50 grams of Gruyère, sliced
Pepper
Nutmeg

———— PREPARATION ————

Preheat the oven to 240 °C. Stir the crème fraiche, add the grated cheese and set aside for ten minutes.

Meanwhile, spread mustard on one side of each slice of bread and add the gammon and slices of Gruyère. Put the halves together and put the cheese and crème fraiche mixture on top. Conclude with a few twists from the pepper mill and some ground nutmeg.

Put it in the oven for 8 minutes. Set the grill at the maximum setting and put the croque under the grill for another 2 to 3 minutes. If you prefer a *croque-madame*, fry an egg sunny-side up in butter while the croque is in the oven and put it on top.

LA VIE EN BEURRE

I once lost my heart to a French chef who'd put an entire pack of butter in the frying pan before he even started to think about what he would cook for us. He proved not to be the only one. Indeed: when, during my first year in Paris, the city suffered from a butter shortage, half the city was in utter panic. This is the story: milk production had declined, while the demand for butter increased after butter started to lose its unhealthy image outside of the French borders. Rightfully so, because as American culinary author and environmental expert Joan Gussow once said: *As for butter versus margarine, I trust cows more than chemists.* As a result, prices soared and the butter shelves in the supermarkets remained empty more often and for longer periods of time. It was an insurmountable drama in a country where butter is considered a vital necessity of life. And so Parisians stocked up large amounts of their favourite butter in their freezers. The habit of keeping butter in one's fridge made me laugh seven years ago, but I must admit that I am now also guilty of keeping a few packs in stock. After all, everything in life is better with butter. Today, butter is the first ingredient to go into my frying pan, and the last. I even put a lump of butter on my freshly made omelettes. Also delicious: some butter on your slices of dried sausage as an appetiser. Or in a bowl of mussels. I could go on forever. *Avec du beurre, tout est meilleur.*

BUTTER COUTURIER

The most famous butter maker in France may be Breton Jean-Yves Bordier. Restaurants that use his butter tend to state this on their menus in giant letters. The secret? Butter by Bordier is extensively kneaded, resulting in a softer structure compared to other butters. After salting, it is manually shaped. It has a full and creamy taste with a hint of nuttiness, which changes slightly with the seasons. So for real butter nutters it's not just about the type of butter, but also about season and origin. The taste depends on the breed of cattle, but also where and when they graze. It shouldn't surprise you that the French distinguish between *beurre d'été* and *beurre d'hiver*. The first – summer butter – is brighter yellow, softer, more aromatic and more popular than winter butter, which is made of milk from cattle that are housed and eat nothing but hay. The texture of winter butter is harder and its flavour not as rich.

Bordier adds seasoning to some of his butters. The variety with *piment d'espellette* – the aromatic chilli from the south-west of France – is in high demand. And his butters with added truffle, yuzu and vanilla are no less delicious. I always buy raspberry butter in summer; a bright pink butter that's only available during the raspberry season. Have it for breakfast with some baguette or put it on a crêpe. In any case: as soon as raspberry butter is on the Parisian shelves you know that summer is here.

BUTTER PURÉE

French dishes usually contain much more butter than you'd think. Mashed potatoes may just be the best example, in particular the legendary version by Joël Robuchon. This French top chef owned restaurants all over the world with a total of over sixty Michelin stars. He is no longer among us, but his mashed potatoes and many other signature dishes from his hands can still be enjoyed at l'Atelier on the Rue de Montalembert. Every chef I know has enjoyed a meal here, because for a long time it was considered a culinary place of pilgrimage. I haven't been there for years, because although the food is exquisite, it's packed with tourists to a point that the allure has somewhat worn off. Fortunately, his mashed potatoes are easily made at home. Be sure to stick to the prescribed amount of butter. In his cookery books, Robuchon indicated a mere 250 grams of butter for a kilo of potatoes, but his restaurants actually use way more than this amount – proportions are even equal, more often than not.

MASHED POTATOES BY ROBUCHON

The type of butter used for this world-famous dish is of crucial importance: cold and preferably unpasteurised and unsalted. Naturally, the quality of potatoes used is also relevant. Robuchon used small La Ratte potatoes cooked unpeeled.

――― SERVES 6

1 kilo of La Ratte potatoes unpeeled
800 grams of unsalted butter, cold and in cubes
10 grams of salt
200 ml full-cream milk
Salt and white pepper
In addition: a passing sieve

――― PREPARATION ―――

Leave the peel on the potatoes. Put them in a pan and submerge them in water. Add the salt and bring to the boil. Lower the heat and boil the potatoes with the lid on the pan for 20 to 25 minutes until done. Drain, allow the steam to evaporate and peel.

Pass the potatoes through a passing sieve. Return to the pan and put over low heat. Add the butter bit by bit while stirring vigorously and quickly – Robuchon used a wooden spoon to do this.

Meanwhile, heat the milk in another small pan. Add the milk gradually to the potatoes once they have stopped taking up butter. You may not need all of it; this depends on how thick you like your mashed potatoes. Add the rest of the butter and flavour with salt and white pepper.

Pass the mashed potatoes through a fine sieve to make it even softer.

A CRASH COURSE IN BUTTER

- In Paris, you buy the best of butter at a *crèmerie* or a *fromagerie*. Some places have giant lumps of butter from which pieces are cut and sold. Most supermarkets also have a wide selection of butters. I once counted 109 varieties at La Grande Épicerie de Paris. One-hundred-and-nine!

- *Beurre fin* is made from pasteurised milk, resulting in a less profound flavour. *Beurre au lait cru* – made from unpasteurised milk – is the better choice with much more flavour. *Beurre de baratte* is also unpasteurised. It's made from cream that has matured a bit longer.

- Salt content is another important characteristic for butter. I only really use the unsalted beurre doux for cooking. *Beurre demi-sel* is lightly salted with a salt content of 0.5 to 3 per cent. My absolute favourite is *beurre salé*, which contains 3 per cent of salt. I especially like *fleur de sel*, because I love the way the grains of salt crunch between your teeth.

- Also take the origin of the butter into account. It's usually stated on the packaging, because the French always like to know where their products come from. *AOP Beurre d'Isigny* is from Normandy, *AOP Beurre de Bresse* from Burgundy and *AOP Beurre Charentes-Poitou* from the Charentes, Poitou and Vendée.

EIGHT HIGH-QUALITY BUTTERS

1. Laurent Dubois supplies the best restaurants in Paris with cheeses, as well as his own butter from Normandy. *47 Boulevard Saint-Germain, 5ᵗʰ* **2.** Good fromageries will cut the butter for you on the spot. I bought this butter at La Souris Gourmande. *5 Rue des Martyrs, 9ᵗʰ* **3.** The raspberry butter by Bordier is only prepared in summer. It's sold at La

Grande Épicerie. *38 Rue de Sèvres, 7th* **4.** Butter by Quatrehomme is soft, salty and delicious. *32 Rue de l'Espérance, 13th* **5.** Slightly spicy and as orange as a Hermès box: butter with *piment d'espellette* by Bordier. Available at La Grande Épicerie. *38 Rue de Sèvres, 7th* **6.** I like my *tartine beurrée* best by far with salted butter by Beillevaire. *77 Rue Saint-Antoine, 4th* **7.** Everything Marie Anne Cantin sells in her cheese shop is fantastic. This also applies to the butter with her name on it. *12 Rue du Champ de Mars, 7th* **8.** The hand-moulded butter by Au Bon Beurre is extremely creamy and easy to spread. Oddly enough I buy it at the greengrocer at *16 Rue des Martyrs, 9th*

4

LE GOÛTER

As with all things Parisian,
presentation is crucial for pastries.
Served on the very best dishes
from the china cabinet, cookies,
cakes and tarts are seldom
eaten casually.

CAKES & CHAMPAGNE

The life which I expected would be too good to be true actually turned out to be even better – and similarly true. For about two years I shuttled between Amsterdam and Paris every other week, the train functioning as my third workplace. Loves came, went and eventually stayed. I had become addicted to the infinite beauty of Paris, its zinc roofs that change colour like an urban sea as the day unfolds. As I would sit writing at my open windows, I realised I wanted to stay in Paris indefinitely.

And so I continued searching for a permanent place to live as a replacement for my temporary rental apartment. This proved to be quite the challenge, because Paris counts more estate agents than bakeries and behind all those impressive Haussmannian façades are rabbit warrens of apartments. Giant front doors would open up to courtyards and improvised stairwells and finally to the rear sections of houses with endlessly split floors. I viewed basement flats without kitchens, dilapidated attic rooms with shared

bathrooms and a strikingly large number of apartments with a view of blind walls. No dream house among them, not even after seeing a hundred houses and apartments. Eventually Alexandra – neurotic, dazzling and chain smoking – came to my rescue. Tired of the fashion scene, she had traded her job at Louis Vuitton for an estate agent's office at the Rue des Martyrs. Unfortunately, she had significantly more talent for fashion: Alexandra would be in front of the office smoking and pretending she was madly busy, but to her frustration she hadn't sold a single house after a year.

On Christmas Eve, our despair was such that we decided to stop our joint quest and pick things up again in January. But first we would take a quick look at an apartment that was due to come on the market the following week. Ten minutes later, I climbed an endless flight of stairs in a building around the corner from me. The attic apartment was previously an artist's studio. Perhaps not very practical, but I was enchanted by its giant windows, wooden floors, limestone walls, the soft light and the view over the roofs of *quartier* Trudaine. So I traded my tiny icy-cold room in the Rue Bochart de Saron for a spacious and searing hot studio two hundred metres away.

After my visit to the notary – who in line with her rate was called Madame Couturier – Alexandra and I finally had something to celebrate. I considered that in addition to champagne, we also deserved cakes. Alexandra kept to the champagne and half a packet of cigarettes, leaving the cake after one courtesy bite. After all, smoking and drinking in the morning is not an issue, but cakes? *Mais non!* If she ever had cake, it would be in the afternoon during *le goûter*. It goes to show – yet again – that most French are disciplined eaters, never indulge in snacks and stick to set times when it comes to eating.

LE QUATRE-HEURES

Le goûter is around 4 pm and can be compared to an afternoon tea, although it's less extensive and, without exception, sweet. It usually consists of a titbit, such as a macaron, a madeleine or a *pain au chocolat*. Crisps? Olives? Unthinkable; that's for the aperitif.

Le goûter is the favourite time of day for children and a cherished tradition even in schools. Adults sometimes meet for *le goûter*, either at home or at one of the many Parisian tearooms. Naturally, the French restrain themselves and often share a cake. After all, it's about the taste; *goûter* translates as 'tasting'.

As with all things Parisian, presentation is crucial here. Served on the very best dishes from the china cabinet, cookies, cakes and tarts are seldom eaten casually. Presentation plays an equally important role in shops: if you buy a cake at one of the many patisseries, it's without exception packaged expertly in a box and custom bag.

MACARONS

My first real pastry love was the macaron. More specifically: the macaron by Pierre Hermé. I tasted it for the first time about twenty years ago, and my timing for this momentous event could not have been better: Hermé had just opened his first shop in Paris and I had just started writing about food. Hermé's macarons are baked perfectly (the egg white slightly crisp at the first bite and then deliciously chewy) and no less revolutionary as regards taste. Hermé combines raspberries and roses, apricots and saffron and – my favourite still – chestnut and green tea which is only available in autumn and winter. Come Christmas time, Hermé prepares macarons with caviar, *foie gras* and champagne, followed in summer by countless combinations with red fruits. His Ispahan – a large rose macaron filled with raspberry, lychee and rose cream – has become world-famous.

Thanks to Hermé, everyone around the world is familiar with macarons. A decade ago you had to search high and low to find them, today it's something of an overkill: virtually every pastry chef sells them and pens, bikinis and phone cases featuring macarons are widely available. And while I do keep a box with macaron Christmas baubles in the attic, I rarely eat them today. Until autumn sets in of course, when Hermé sells his chestnut macarons.

THREE BEST MACARONS IN PARIS

1. The chestnut and green tea macarons by **Pierre Hermé**
2. The chocolate macarons by **Jean-Paul Hévin**
3. The rose and cardamom macarons by **Ladurée**

OF OLD MASTERS & INSTAGRAM STARS

Naturally, there's way more to pastry than just macarons. I haven't really counted them, but word has it that Paris has over 30,000 bakeries and patisseries. You come across a window displaying cakes and tarts on almost every street corner, each one even more beautiful than the last. While the rest of the world may occasionally buy a cake at a supermarket, Parisians are far less inclined to do so. *À chacun son métier*, the French say, or: each to their own. Pastry is considered to be an important craft. This is also the reason why classic French chefs hesitate to prepare cakes and pastry themselves. Instead, they are more comfortable hiring a pastry chef or working with a good pastrycook in the vicinity of their restaurant. Parisian hotels follow their example. From the Ritz to the Bristol: all top hotels employ pastry chefs or chocolatiers who are given all the space and budget required to develop, making for wonderful *le goûter* experiences.

LES SAISONS

The seasons play a significant role where Parisian top pastry chefs are concerned: more often than not, you can tell the time of year by their cakes and tarts. It never ceases to amaze and impress me, probably because in any other part of the world even the best of pastry chefs sell strawberry cake all year round. This is simply unthinkable in Paris. Claire

Damon, one of the best female pastry chefs in this city, goes even further selling cakes made with *mara de bois* – tiny wild strawberries – in summer in her shop Des Gâteaux et du Pain. You can see the seasons change in windows of most other pastry chefs too. June features cakes and tarts with cherries, July with peaches. In August, pastry chefs use apricots and Reine Claudes and in winter it's impossible to get around the Mont Blancs: cakes made from meringue and covered with whipped cream and trails of chestnut purée.

TWELVE MILLION FOLLOWERS

Parisians are generally extremely visually orientated, but where patisserie is concerned they manage to outdo themselves. In recent years they might have gone to extremes, mainly because of Instagram. Trends are rampant and the new creations from young pastry chefs go viral on a regular basis, causing some of them to achieve rock-star status. The ultimate example is Cédric Grolet, who has over twelve million followers on Instagram. He initially made his name at Hotel Le Meurice with his signature trompe-l'œil cakes: glossy, perfectly reproduced fruits, such as pomegranates, lemons, apples and pears, to be eaten whole. When a few years later Grolet opened a shop at the Avenue de l'Opéra, on the very first day there was a queue long enough for me to miss my train twice. Another big name of the new generation is François Perret of the Ritz. Similar to Grolet, everything he creates is as beautiful and colourful as it is instagrammable.

HEROES

No matter how ravishing the creations by these popular pastry chefs, their taste does not always come close to competing with the old masters. Take the cakes by classic French experts such as Philippe Conticini and, in particular, Pierre Hermé and Jacques Genin. Although their creations are perhaps somewhat less visually spectacular, after just one bite you'll know exactly why they remain in a class of their own.

Hermé's flavours are always original, yet subdued and perfectly balanced. Also, his patisserie is technically perfect and his *millefeuille* may just be the best I have ever had. His tarte infinement vanille with three different vanilla varieties for an infinitely layered vanilla taste – hence the name – is definitely something you should try.

Then there are those maddeningly delicious cakes by Jacques Genin, but these are actually quite hard to get because Genin boasts about freshness to the extent that he exclusively works *à la minute*. If you'd like to taste one of his cakes, be sure to order them one day in advance. Alternatively, you might go to his shop on a Saturday morning at 11 am, when he prepares a small supply. Be sure to try his lemon cake, which is one of the freshest and most elegant cakes I have ever had. His Paris-Brest – a garland of pastry dough filled with soft, sweet hazelnut cream – is famous. It was invented by French pastry chef Louis Durnand in honour of the Paris-Brest cycling race; hence its wheel-shaped form. Almost every pastry chef sells them, but Genin's is considered the very best.

THE NEW SWEET

There is a new generation of pastry chefs who are not at all bothered about Instagram hits, but instead focus on flavours. Their patisserie is generally not as sweet and they make ample use of ingredients that used to be inconceivable for patisserie. The best example is Tapisserie, which is owned by Septime, one of the best restaurants in the world. This is where you'll find choux pastry with bee pollen and cream with hay. Their tarte à l'erable is well on its way to becoming a new Paris classic. Made with maple syrup and whipped cream, it may not be as photogenic as the cakes by, for instance, Cedric Grolet, but it certainly is much tastier.

Finally: the best development in recent years is the rise of Asian patisserie. A few names to remember are Vietnamese Caphette in the 11th and Japanese Mori Yoshida in the 7th. It just goes to show that you will never run out of delectable things to sample in Paris.

EIGHT PARISIAN CAKES

1. The fruit tarts by Cédric Grolet have reached global fame in a just a few years. *6 Rue de Castiglione, 1st* **2.** If it's just the one tart you will try in Paris, be sure to make it the tarte infinement vanille by Pierre Hermé. *72 Rue Bonaparte, 6th* **3.** Almost every pastry chef sells their own version of the Mont Blanc, but the best ones are sold by Angelina. The shape of this tart was inspired by the bob line hairstyle that was a trend in Paris in the early 20th

century. *226 Rue de Rivoli, 1st* **4.** The more layers in a millefeuille, the better it tastes. This one is by Jacques Genin. *33 Rue de Turenne, 3rd* **5.** The *baba au rum* is rum-soaked cake, invented by Stohrer; the oldest patisserie in the city. *51 Rue Montorgueil, 2nd* **6.** Claire Damon van Des Gâteaux et du Pain prepares cakes with seasonal fruits. This one is with grapefruit. *89 Rue du Bac, 7th* **7.** Never visit Paris without having a lemon tart. The one by Sébastien Gaudard is creamy and fresh sourish. *22 Rue des Martyrs, 9th* **8.** The Paris-Brest was invented in honour of the cycling race of the same name. This one is by Philippe Conticini. *37 Rue de Varenne, 7th*.

PUFFS OF HAPPINESS

If you could do with something sweet but don't want to eat too much, simply treat yourself to some *chouqettes*; French sugared choux pastries that are sold by most boulangeries. They do not remotely resemble those soggy and cloyingly sweet cream-filled factory-made monstrosities that were served at your great-aunt's birthday. No. Chouquettes are airy and slightly sweet puffs of happiness. Their simplest and most delicious version comes unfilled, covered with a sprinkle of pearl sugar.

In Paris, they are usually sold in batches of ten, although there are places where you can buy them one at a time. Handy, because they are best when eaten immediately. I have tried taking them on the train or plane, but this is not a very good idea, because the pearl sugar comes off and the dough softens. The only option is to eat them as soon as you buy them, unless you make your own, which is much easier than you think.

CHOUQUETTES

———————————————————————————— SERVES 4

125 ml of water
125 ml of full-cream milk
1 good pinch of salt
1 teaspoon of sugar
100 grams of butter,
    in small lumps

150 grams of flour
4 eggs, beaten
Pearl sugar
Extra: baking paper,
    piping bag

——————————————— PREPARATION ———————————————

Preheat the oven to 180 °C. Use a saucepan to make the dough. Put the salt, sugar and butter with the water and heat until the butter is melted. Add the flour all at once and stir quickly and vigorously to a smooth batter that easily comes off the pan.

Leave to cool for two minutes and continue by adding the eggs one by one. Stir well.

Put the dough in a piping bag and pipe small balls the size of a walnut onto a baking tray lined with baking paper and leaving plenty of space between them. If you don't have a piping bag, you can use two spoons to make balls.

Brush them with egg yolk and sprinkle with a generous amount of pearl sugar. It must look like it's too much sugar, because the balls will expand while baking. Bake in the oven for 20 minutes or until golden brown.

ALSO SMALL AND EXQUISITE

1. **Tuiles** Boulangerie Dupuy sells the best. If the weather is warm and moist, Madame Dupuy simply won't prepare her almond-orange *tuiles* because they won't be crisp enough. Poor consolation: Monsieur Dupuy bakes a fabulous tarte tatin. *13 Rue Cadet, 9th*

2. **Madeleines** Buttery shell-shaped cakes, ridged on one side and spherical on the other. Cyril Lignac sells really good ones. *2 Rue de Chaillot, 16th*

3. **Wagashi** Parisians love the Japanese feel for aesthetics, and I feel very fortunate that Paris is dotted with shops selling Japanese sweet products. Toroya sells the best *wagashi*. *10 Rue Saint-Florentin, 1st*

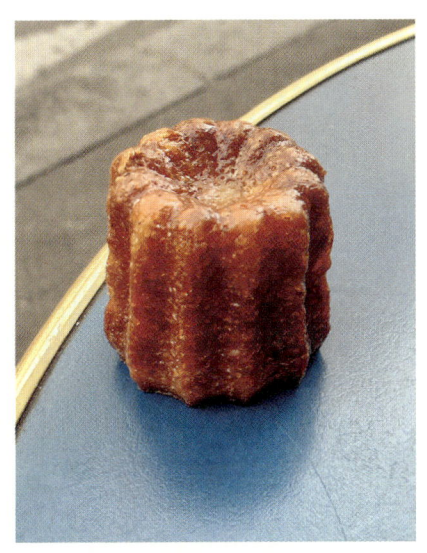

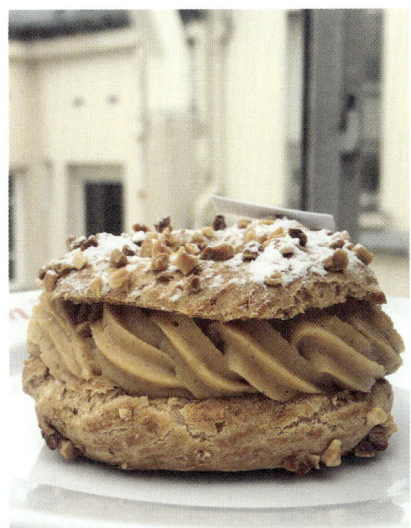

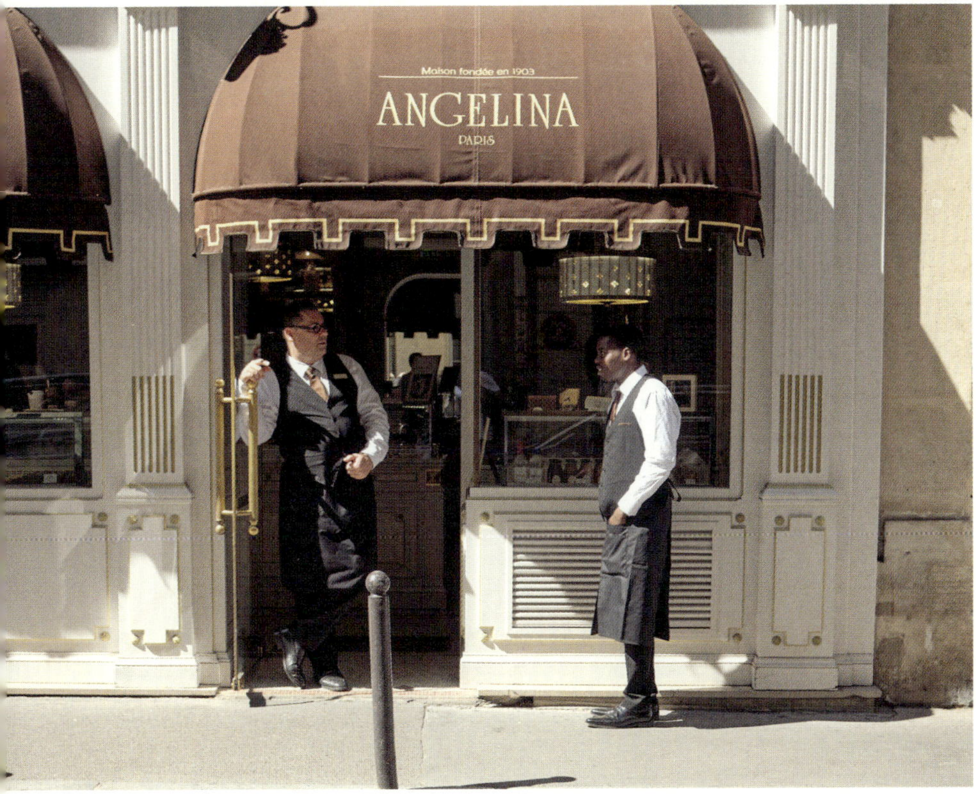
Maison fondée en 1903
ANGELINA
PARIS

LE THÉ

With the odd exception, Parisians drink tea during *le goûter*. This, as may come to no surprise, is seldom merely a cup of tea. In addition to the countless tearooms, most the hotels and restaurants in the city have tea menus and use the most beautiful porcelain to serve their tea. Paris is heaving with tea shops, so you can drink the very best at home. One predicable consequence: after seven years in Paris, half of the space in my pantry is taken up by tea. I started with a collection of tea tins by the very old (established in 1854!) tea shop Mariage Frères – because they are just, well, stunning. Their Fantôme de l'Opéra is still one of my favourites: a green tea flavoured with grapefruit, orange, lemon, ginger, rose petals and blue flowers. Once poured, it takes on this magical bluish green colour. They have various establishments in Paris, but the one at Rue du Bourg Tibourg also serves *le goûter*. *30 rue du Bourg Tibourg, 4th*

JAPANESE TEMPLE

Still, it's not all French tearooms in Paris; because Parisians have this great fondness for tea, other tea cultures are given plenty of space and opportunity. I have meanwhile expanded my tea collection and frequent different addresses for all of my tea varieties. Ogata is the very summit for Japanese tea. It's one of the most serene and beautiful places in the Marais where they serve lunch and dinner. They also sell tea and hold tea ceremonies. These extensive tea tastings are combined with very small yet refined and sophisticated bites. I once had a three-year-old tea served with dried kaki and butter; an unrivalled combination.
16 Rue Debelleyme, 3rd

MOROCCAN OASIS

The enchanting courtyard of La Grande Mosquée de Paris presents an altogether different setting. Here, they serve mint tea exactly as it should be. Order some delicious Arabic patisserie and – for enthusiasts – a water pipe. Don't skip the venue just because you are a tea sceptic, because the largest mosque in Paris is worth a visit in itself.
2 Place du Puits de l'Ermite, 5th

CHINESE ICONS

You really should visit one or two Chinese tearooms. I have two favourites. The first one is the tea shop of starred restaurant Yam'Tcha in Rue Sauval. Whether you come for just one cup of tea or an entire tasting, be sure to order a bao with cherries and Stilton, because you'll never find these steamed rolls any fluffier than here.
Sweet tooths take it to the great T'Xuan, featuring a marvellous blend of chic Chinese Parisiennes and families with children enjoying all those tea varieties and, in particular, the spectacular desserts. I am simply addicted to their *bingsu* with mango and their velvety tofu cheesecake.
4 Rue Sauval, 1e & 56 Rue La Fayette, 9th

THE ART OF CHOCOLATE

Chocolate milk is another serious matter in Paris. In 1615, it was introduced as an exclusive novelty on the occasion of the marriage between Louis XIII and Anne of Austria. For years, chocolate was exclusively consumed in its liquid form and served at courts and in aristocratic circles, with sugar and vanilla or cinnamon. Marie-Antoinette, Louis XVI's wife, loved it to the extent that she hired a chocolate maker with the official title of Le Chocolatier de la Reine. This chocolatier experimented extensively with new flavour combinations, such as hot chocolate with orange blossom and sweet almonds.

The biggest fan, however, was without a doubt Louis XV, who had a great heart for women and hot chocolate alike. Not a coincidence maybe, seeing as aphrodisiac qualities were attributed to chocolate in those early days. Royal lovers Madame de Pompadour and Madame du Barry used to drink it constantly in an attempt to keep up with the king's extravagant libido.

Over the centuries, it has become a common drink for everyone, although in Paris it's still associated with luxury to this day. Ordering a *chocolat chaud* is quite a chic thing to do. The creamy drink served in Paris is in sharp contrast with its counterpart served with whipped cream in some other countries. I'm not likely to ever forget the first time I drank it. It cost

CHOCOLAT CHAUD

When you set out to prepare your own hot chocolate, there is one crucial thing to consider: never use cocoa powder. Instead, buy a bar of dark chocolate of the best quality you can find, preferably containing at least 70% cocoa solids.

ERGIBT 2 TASSEN

350 ml full-cream milk
220 grams of chocolate, chopped
150 ml cream
2 teaspoons of sugar

PREPARATION

Heat the milk, cream and sugar in a saucepan with a thick bottom and stir in the chocolate. If you are not used to the French penchant for fat, you can skip the cream and use more milk instead.

Serve with extra full-cream milk to thin the drink. Also delicious with a pinch of *fleur de sel*.

15 euros. It was served in a white porcelain cup and was almost syrupy. Next to it was a silver jug with more milk to dilute the chocolate syrup as desired. The result? A liquid cake instead of hot chocolate. A creamy substance with an intense, subtly sweet and slightly bitter chocolate taste. It took one sip to realise that it wasn't that expensive at all and two sips to know for sure that this was the best money I'd ever spent. And above all: that the Parisian good life and *chocolat chaud* are indissolubly linked.

If you want to taste some of the best, you might consider going to a hotel such as the Ritz or Le Meurice, but the most iconic venue is Angelina. In 1903, Austrian pastry chef Anton Rumpelmayer established this tearoom which he named after his daughter-in-law. It was a second home to Coco Chanel (interesting fact: she used to sit at table 10) and Marcel Proust also frequented the venue. Today, however, you will find an endless number of tourists waiting in line for a table to become available. Most Parisians know how to circumvent the queue by skipping the tearoom itself and instead using the shop entrance where they order their *chocolat chaud à emporter* – to take away. After buying some, cross over to Le Jardin de Tuileries across the street and sit down on a bench there to enjoy unsurpassed hot chocolate and an equally unsurpassed view. *226 Rue de Rivoli, 1st*

EASTER EGGS

So the love of chocolate did not remain restricted to kings and mistresses and Paris evolved into a paradise for chocolate fans. Chocolatiers are considered artists; sometimes even literally, as in the case of Patrick Roger who creates these giant chocolate sculptures. I love gazing at his shop windows, certainly at Easter time. The chocolate Easter egg – this should have occurred to you by now – was invented in Paris in the eighteenth century. Soon after, pastry chefs naturally turned creating the most richly decorated egg in the city into a sport. This has never changed. Even hotels go all out, and chocolatier Johan Giacchetti of Le Bristol has enjoyed particular success. But then, there is much at stake here: every year, French *Vogue* still selects the most beautiful specimens in the city, and Giacchetti is almost always on its list.

DUCASSE

Chocolate enthusiasts do not have to wait until Easter to indulge in delicious chocolate. Paris is home to an incredible number of good chocolatiers, one of them Jacques Genin. His daughter Jade has also made chocolate her life's work and she's rapidly evolving into the new chocolate genius of Paris. Another favourite is Jean-Paul Hévin. Everything he creates has a highly intense chocolate taste, and his chocolate éclair in particular has enhanced his reputation. Éclair actually translates into a lightning flash, and its shape and flavour ensure it exceeds the speed of light.

Nevertheless, I generally buy my chocolate from the same premises: the chocolate shop of top chef Alain Ducasse. I really wouldn't know how many bars I have devoured, but it must be a shocking number. The fact that the packaging is irresistible and the number of outlets has increased immensely over the last few years really does not help at all. The best shop still is his little chocolate factory in the Rue de la Roquette where you can see how he creates his chocolate.

♀ THREE FAVOURITES

Chocolate Alain Ducasse Don't hesitate to buy one of the bars with praline and *fleur de sel*. *40 Rue de la Roquette, 11th*
Louis Fouquet Chocolatier and confectioner, or a specialist in candying fruit and other sweets. Be sure to taste the *oranginettes*: candied orange peel in pure chocolate. *46 Rue du Bac, 7th*
Jade Genin Emerging chocolate talent and daughter of Jacques Genin. Already famous in culinary circles for her magnificent Easter eggs. *33 Avenue de l'Opéra, 1st*

HOW TO BECOME A
CHOCOLATE SNOB

- Stay away from chocolate in any supermarket and buy exclusively from chocolatiers.

- Note the origin: packaging on high-end chocolate states the origin of the cocoa beans used. Try chocolate from different countries to learn to taste the subtle differences.

- Taste like a pro: start by looking at its colour. Is it dark or light? Can you make out other hues in the brown? Continue by examining its structure. Is if hard or soft, and does it melt quickly in your hands? After that, break off a piece and listen to the sound. Smell the chocolate to note its various flavours. And, last but not least, taste it. Chew well, move it around in your mouth and note flavours as well as structure.

- Try chocolate with increasing cocoa percentages. The higher the percentage, the less sugar and milk it contains, which brings out more of that real chocolate flavour.

- Not a fan of dark chocolate? Simply start with 40 per cent cocoa percentage and gradually increase it. Some chocolatiers even make bars with 100 per cent cocoa. This mighty sensation may require some getting used to, but once you have, you can explore the taste of exquisite, layered flavours and bitter fruit.

GLACE PARISIENNE

There's no place in the world with more magnificent and impressive ice-cream desserts and cakes than Paris, of which the latter are true showpieces for the after-dinner table at home. After all, why go to the trouble of making ice cream yourself when the country's best *glaciers* are a mere stone's throw from your house? At Berthillon, the oldest in the city, they sell a luscious ice cream tarte tatin, which even comes with caramelised apple. Equally sumptuous is the soft pink Bombe Glacée Alexandra; a giant ball of peach sorbet filled with champagne ice cream.

The Parisian ice-cream scene has provided ample room for new flavours. Take Lebanese ice-cream parlours Glace Bachir and Bältis, which have been indisputable successes for many years. Personally I swear by the ice cream from Café Isaka, where they sell these great Asian flavours, such as pandan. Oh, and don't hesitate to enjoy some of that Japanese shaved ice served in summer, available at Toraya or Hexagone.

Similar to patisseries, a new generation of *glaciers* has emerged that use less cream and remarkably little sugar. Fruttini, for instance, sells fruits filled with sorbet, such as a pineapple filled with pineapple sorbet or a gigantic cocoa pod filled with chocolate ice cream; the ultimate eyecatcher to finish a home-cooked dinner with friends. Another favourite is Jacques Genin, who I have already mentioned. He prepares his ice cream *à la minute* with hardly any sugar. So don't worry if you enter his shop and don't see any ready-made ice cream, because it's not prepared until ordered. And you should know that in summer his daughter Jade prepares a mean granita in her shop on the Avenue de l'Opéra.

The most fun address for some delicious ice cream is without a doubt Folderol; a wine bar and ice-cream parlour combined. This may sound peculiar, but works like a charm. From late afternoon until late at night, the place is packed with Parisians and other oenophiles in an ever-exuberant atmosphere. And yes, this also makes it the perfect venue to enjoy your aperitif.

♥ THREE FAVOURITES

Folderol For the equally improbable yet fantastic combination of a glass of wine and some ice cream. *Rue du Grand Prieuré, 11th*
Fruttini The most beautiful, fruity and light ice cream in the city. I like the avocado variant best. *24 Rue Saint-Placide, 6th*
Café Isaka Ice cream that features Asian flavours, such as ube, pandan and sesame. Be sure to taste their coffees. *9 Rue Thérèse, 1st*

5

L'APÉRO

Parisians have mastered the art of the aperitif like no other, and you'll find wine bars and cafés packed between six and eight in the evening.

THE FRENCH
WINE LOBBY

Despite the COVID pandemic, my fourth year in Paris might just have been the best year ever. France found itself in a harsh lockdown: trains weren't operating and borders were closed. People weren't allowed to enter France, even if they owned a house there. After years of shuttling, it also kind of felt like a relief: there was a certain advantage in having to stay in Amsterdam uninterrupted for a time, not rushing to catch the train every Friday and not living two lives instead of one. Naturally, it took just a few months before my desire to go to my home in Paris became excruciating. I wanted to know how everyone was doing, check on my apartment and, most importantly, I wanted to see with my own eyes whether French gastronomy could actually be halted and put on pause. Following an e-mail exchange with the embassy, I was permitted to cross the border by car, armed with my press card and a folder filled with COVID forms. I found Paris to be even quieter than Amsterdam. In fact, the lights were actually switched off at Au Pied de Cochon – the brasserie that had gained global fame because it's normally open 24 hours a day. It was as frightening as it was astonishing. The boulevards were desolate and the lack of exhaust fumes had allowed for a fragrance I had never smelled in Paris before: that of spring. I had never seen the Parisian air so blue, the streets so beautiful or experienced the quiet quite so… silent. Despite all the misery COVID had inflicted upon us, it also brought about an ultimate luxury: for the first time ever, Paris was exclusively for Parisians. I went to the Louvre and found I had entire rooms to myself. I could easily sit and admire a painting for a quarter of an hour; the same painting that would normally require you to stand in line for ages. I sauntered through the empty corridors that, after decades of uninterrupted bustle, had now fallen quiet. Paris was granted the opportunity to recharge, and so was I.

The bacchanals, the lavish dinners, all these came to a standstill. Instead, a curfew was instituted and restaurants and cafés were closed. However, the popularity of takeaway menus didn't catch on as it did in cities such as Amsterdam. Alain Ducasse explained the reason why in *The New York Times*: 'Having a meal delivered and eating it in the kitchen does not portray the good life at all. People want to share a bottle of good wine in good company. They want to see other people, beautifully dressed, instead of just their partner across the kitchen table.' And so the roll-down shutters of Parisian hotels and restaurants remained closed.

APERUES

Despite all this upset, the French joie de vivre found its way, as always, albeit in alternative ways. In the early evenings in particular, Parisians would come out into the streets en masse to enjoy an aperitif together before curfew at eight. This resulted in *aperues*: streets would fill with people, bottles and glasses, more often than not near cafés that were naturally not permitted to receive guests, but did offer take-away menus. Contrary to

all advice, the squares, avenues and quaysides of the Seine and the Canal Saint-Martin filled up with people.

It was quite a remarkable phenomenon, because most French are law-abiding citizens who generally strictly complied with other COVID measures. The police turned a blind eye, probably because the *aperues* were more about maintaining French traditions and not so much a sign of resistance per se. However these *aperues* proved to be new sources of infection. Macron even decided to bring the curfew forward to six o'clock, *'pour contrer l'effet apéro.'* It was to no avail: people would then meet in the streets by five. Because meeting in the house was not an option due to the risk of contamination, my neighbour Sebastian and I would secretly drink our wine outside in the street. After all: a fine is preferable to no aperitif any time.

VACCINATION PRIORITY

When the first COVID vaccine was introduced, French winemakers demanded priority in the vaccination rounds. Their reasoning: if they were to lose their sense of taste, this would have formidable consequences for the quality of their wines and the entire country. French gastronomy was at stake, they argued. They were the very same winemakers who a few years before had loudly protested when the government started a campaign to promote dry January. How dare the government stigmatise drinking alcohol and endanger French culture? Many chefs declared war on dry January. Alain Ducasse expressed his objection by giving considerable discounts on his best wines for the entire month. His action had a significant effect: swayed by a strong wine lobby, Macron decided to break off the campaign.

THE ONLY VINEYARD IN PARIS

It may be clear by now that it is not wise to trifle with the French and alcohol, and Parisians naturally hold great feelings for their one and only vineyard: Le Vigne du Clos Montmartre, just behind the Sacré-Coeur. If you didn't know any better, you'd imagine that this mini vineyard measuring less than 500 square metres had been there since time immemorial. Nothing could be further from the truth. It used to be a dump, until the 1940s when the city council decided to plant a vineyard to prevent the ground from being acquired by project developers. Nonetheless, harvest festivals are held there that make it seem as if they are an ancient tradition. La Fête des Vendanges is usually scheduled in early October and lasts for five days. The festivities are much more extensive than the vineyard itself and the quality of the wine is not all that. Not a problem, because you can easily obtain really good wine anywhere else in Paris.

♀ THREE FAVOURITES

Septime La Cave Heaven on earth for natural wine fanatics. *3 Rue Basfroi, 11th*
Le Barav This always cheerful local tavern in the Marais serves excellent charcuterie. *6 Rue Charles-François Dupuis, 3rd*
Frenchie Bar à Vins Brother of the famous restaurant Frenchie owned by chef Grégory Marchand. *6 Rue du Nil, 2nd*

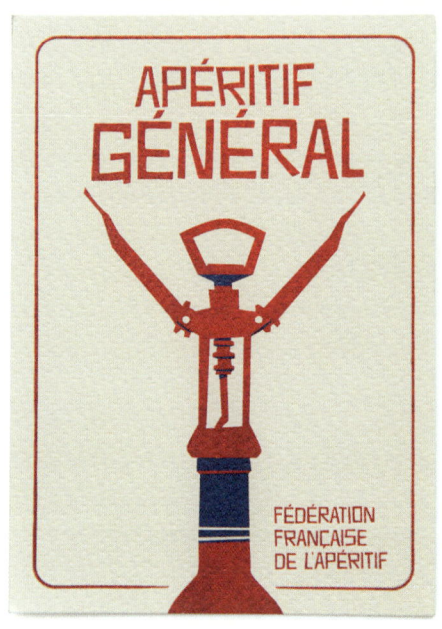

PRENDRE UN VERRE

Under normal circumstances, *l'heure de l'apéro* starts at about 6 to 7 pm; too early for dinner and too late to do anything meaningful, which really leaves just one option: to sit, relax and zone out for a bit with a glass of wine, a beer or a cocktail, a few olives and some good charcuterie. This moment of stillness, the ultimate idleness, the knowledge that the day is over and the promise of a meal ahead is my favourite time of the day – at least since I moved to Paris.

The French have mastered the art of the aperitif like no other. Those who consider dining before 8 pm are in for disappointment because they'll find most restaurants are still closed. The wine bars and cafés, however, will be packed at that time: masses of people meet for drinks, or, in French: *prendre un verre* (literally: 'taking a glass'). An aperitif is not just a glass before dinner, it's a ritual.

The idea of the aperitif is not to become intoxicated. On the contrary, it's meant to relax you before having a meal, and stimulate the appetite. It has an even more important function for people having guests for dinner: it provides just that little more time to finish things in the kitchen and gives latecomers a little extra time.

Naturally, the *apéro* is not merely about drinks, food is also a part of it. Cafés generally serve olives or nuts between 6 and 8 pm, or even a complete board of salted snacks known as *grignotages salés*. The only thing you need for a home aperitif is an extensive stock of delicatessen treats. In Paris, all I have to do is walk around the corner to my local supermarket which has a special shelf for the aperitif, consisting of prepacked charcuterie, *mélanges apéro* and *biscuits apéro*. Specialist shops sell the best non-perishable items in jars and cans. I even have an old baker's display case at home filled to the brim with aperitif snacks.

If you can't find the time to go to ten different specialist shops, not to worry. Simply head for the FFA: Fédération Française de l'Apéritif, a true ode to the aperitif. From marinated mussels to speciality beers and champagnes to jeu-de-boules sets, they sell everything you need for that perfect Parisian *apéro. 2 Rue de Paradis, 10th, 50 Rue des Dames, 17th and 18 Rue des Martyrs, 9th*

RADIS AU BEURRE

A delicacy regularly served during aperitifs: radishes with beurre maître d'hôtel. The softness and creaminess of the butter combined with the crispness and slight bitterness of radish is a match made in heaven.

SERVES 4

100 grams of the best quality butter you can find
3 tablespoons of finely chopped shallot
3 tablespoons of finely chopped parsley
1 teaspoon of lemon juice
3 bunches of radishes
If you are using unsalted butter: half a teaspoon of salt

PREPARATION

Prepare the *beurre maître d'hôtel* by combining all the ingredients except for the radishes and transfer the butter mixture to some plastic foil. Make a roll of about 10 centimetres long and put it in the freezer. Cut the radishes from the bunches and serve with the butter, and some baguette too, if you like.

A CRASH COURSE IN APÉRO

- Aperitif is derived from the Latin *aperire*, which means to open up. An aperitif opens up one's appetite. In France, the abbreviation *apéro* is generally used.

- *L'heure de l'apéro* literally means the aperitif hour and is usually sometime between 6 and 8 pm.

- *Prendre un verre* means having a drink. Also referred to as *boire un coup*.

- A board with aperitif snacks such as charcuterie, olives and pickled vegetables is referred to as a *planche apéro*. It's also called a *planche à partager* – a board for sharing.

- Be sure to have something in stock for aperitif at all times. Examples include tins of sardines, jars with terrine, rillettes or pâté. Dry-cured sausage, preferably served with some butter and cornichons on the side, are perfect. Finally, be sure to stock up on a good nut mix. French supermarkets sell special *mélanges apéro*, but you can also roast some yourself.

- An *apéritif dînatoire* is the extended version of the aperitif, converting it to something more of a dinner. It often takes the form of a buffet-like meal or picnic.

- If all this has made you a fan of the aperitif, you can now officially call yourself an *apérophile*.

CHAMPAGNE
TOUS LES JOURS

It is, has been and always will be the ultimate aperitif, certainly in Paris: champagne. A festive start to dinner, it'll leave you tipsy in a pleasant kind of way. Or, in the words of Madame de Pompadour: *le champagne, c'est le seul vin qui laisse la femme belle après boire*, which translates to 'champagne is the only wine that leaves women beautiful after drinking'. In Parisian restaurants, nobody will frown when you order a glass of bubbles without celebrating something. It's also perfectly acceptable to open a bottle of sparkling wine when you're having some friends over for dinner. It doesn't necessarily have to be champagne: you can choose from a wide selection of affordable alternatives, such as a crémant de Bourgogne.

Always make sure to open a bottle correctly; sparkling wine should never plop when opened. Not because it's considered slightly vulgar, but because it's a shame. Not only will the plop spill some of the wine, but some of the carbonic acid will also dissipate and bubbles will be lost.

The trick is to remove the upper part of the bottle's capsule. Continue by opening the muselet; the wire on the cork. Do this with your right hand and block the cork with your left. The risk of the cork coming loose at this time is slim, but still. Then hold the bottle at a 45-degree angle. Keep holding the cork firmly with your left hand and twist the bottle away from the cork with the right until the bottle opens. Do this gently. In the best of circumstances you will hear a tiny sigh of air when the cork comes loose. Hold the bottle at its base and pour the wine slowly and gently. Don't pour it out all at once, but just a bit at a time. Wait for the froth to come down and pour some more. You can prevent frothing by tilting the glass a little. Don't forget to turn the bottle slightly when putting it upright again; this will prevent leakage.

And, last but not least: hold your glass by its stem and never by its wide end so the temperature of this delicious drink remains stable.

♥ MUST-HAVE: VINTAGE CHAMPAGNE COUPES

Purists consider it not done to drink champagne from a coupe, because it allows the carbonic acid to dissipate more easily. Yet there are plenty of brasseries and restaurants in Paris where champagne is still poured into traditional coupes. Why? Well, it just looks so much more elegant. Can't argue with that! So buy yourself a set of lovely coupes at a *brocante* – a flea market. Go to *www.brocabrac.fr/75* for more information about where and when *brocante* markets are scheduled in Paris.

A CRASH COURSE IN CHAMPAGNE

- A distinction is made between *demi-sec*, *brut* and *extra brut*. Demi-sec champagne contains more sugar, leaving a rather sweet flavour. Brut champagne is drier and contains no more than 15 grams of sugar per litre. I am particularly fond of *extra brut*, a very dry champagne that contains no more than 6 grams of sugar per litre.

- Champagne is generally made from three grape varieties: Chardonnay, Pinot Noir, Meunier, or a blend of these. Four more varieties are permitted, but you seldom come across them.

- *Blanc de Blancs* is exclusively made from Chardonnay grapes; a light champagne with many acids. *Blanc de Noirs* are made from black grapes: Pinot Noir, Meunier or a blend. They are richer in taste with dark fruit tones. Red wine is added to obtain rosé champagne, resulting in a pink colour and a slightly fruity flavour.

- Champagne comes with and without vintage. A champagne without vintage is referred to as *champagne sans millésime*, must have spent about fifteen months maturing and have a stable character and flavour. *Champagne millésime* may take on a variety of features and characters. Grapes used are harvested in a specific year and are left to mature in in the winemaker's cellar for at least three years.

- Do not keep your champagne in the fridge for too long or the cork will dry out. Instead, cool it for about four hours before drinking it, ideally between 8 to 10 °C, but this may vary depending on the variety. Check the label for more information. Forgot to cool the champagne? No worries; simply put your bubbles in a cooler filled with iced water for thirty minutes.

OTHER FAVOURITES

Citron pressé
The choice in non-alcohol drinks is increasing all over the world, and Paris is no exception. A positive development, but the perfect non-alcoholic beverage has actually been here for as long as I can remember: *citron pressé*. I drink it almost daily. It is served in a glass with 50 to 70 ml of fresh lemon juice. It comes with a carafe of water to dilute the juice and some sugar and ice cubes for you to prepare your drink exactly as you like it. I usually skip the sugar. It's served in virtually every café and also in the morning, but I prefer it in the afternoon and during aperitif – especially if I have an extensive dinner planned for later.

Cooled red
In France, cooled red wine is much more common than in other countries. Instead of a cooled white wine or rosé, try a glass of cool red wine for a change. These are generally rather light wines made from Pinot Noir, Gamay or Granache, for instance. I like Brouilly best, preferably by Jean Claude Lapalu.

Kir
I'm not a fan of sweet beverages, but Kir definitely deserves a place in this list. This classic among aperitifs was named after Félix Kir, former Mayor of Dijon. It's made by mixing two tablespoons of crème de cassis and Aligoté or another white wine. Kir Royale substitutes the white wine with crémant de Bourgogne, a sparkling wine. The drink is served in a flute.

Pastis
This anise-flavoured drink is particularly popular in the south of France, but in summer it is also very popular with Parisians. It's made from star anise, liquorice and herbal extracts. With an alcohol percentage of 45 per cent, diluting is imperative. Serve it with one part of Pastis, four parts of ice-cold water and plenty of ice. It's still a bit too strong for me, but die-hards take one or two of these every afternoon, no exceptions. After all, as the French saying goes: *quatre heures moins le quart, l'heure du Ricard!* (Quarter to four, time for Ricard!)

LE PIQUE-NIQUE

It's not uncommon for the *apéro* to evolve into an entirely different and larger event: an *apéritif dînatoire* – an aperitif and meal combined. In summer, these *apéritifs dînatoire* are often in the form of a picnic. No surprises there, because in Paris gardens are virtually non-existent and the balconies barely provide room for two. Now you know why the parks, squares and banks of the river Seine and the Canal Saint-Martin are frequented by masses of people out on a picnic.

Soon after I moved to Paris, picnics were exuberantly celebrated during *Le Dîner en Blanc: a grand apéritif dînatoire* that drew hundreds of people. Everyone was dressed in white and took their own tables, chairs, tableware and a picnic basket. The location would remain secret, because officially it's not permitted to occupy a public space with hundreds of tables to have extensive meals.

I received an e-mail a few hours before the event stating that I had to be ready at 7 pm on the Place Vendôme, from where we would go to our destination. I had no idea how it was managed organisationally, but hundreds of people dressed in white emerged from every corner of the city at the agreed time with folding tables and gigantic picnic baskets, heading to the square in front of the Louvre and the Tuileries. In no time at all, Chinese lanterns were suspended from the trees, tables set with linen, candles lit and glasses filled. The tables were decorated with bottles of excellent wine, large trays with beautiful salads, boards with sausage and the best cheeses to be found in the city. We ate, drank and danced until late.

THE BEST PLACES FOR A PICNIC

Popular venues for a picnic in Paris include the quays of the river Seine and Champs-de-Mars – the park in front of the Eiffel tower. If you are looking for a location more tranquil by the water, consider the Quai de la Loire in the 19th. It's also located by the river Seine, and often surrounded by Parisians playing jeu-de-boule. The undulating Parc des Buttes Chaumont in the same arrondissement is also highly recommended. If you'd rather not sit on the ground, you might venture out to the Jardin du Luxembourg in the 6th that features tables and chairs for public use. The chairs were designed especially for this park and have become world-famous.

PICNIC LIKE A PARISIAN

- Forget about white wine, because in summer it'll be too warm too soon, and fewer things are as bad as lukewarm white wine. Bring cooled red wine instead, which is also good when not that cool anymore.

- Don't bother cooking. Instead, go to a few specialist shops to stock up on some charcuterie, cheese, nuts, a crisp baguette and some cherries or other fruit of the season. If you are planning a more extensive picnic, you might involve one of the many caterers in the city.

- There are plenty of addresses where you can order a picnic basket if you don't feel like doing the shopping yourself. One example is the brasserie Le Grand Colbert. *2 Rue Vivienne, 2nd*

- Since we are talking about Paris, everything has to look tiptop, also when you are eating outdoors. Fortunately, delicatessen items are always packaged in beautiful wrappers, so plates aren't required. With regard to wine glasses: anything is better than plastic cups. Better to ask at a café nearby if you can borrow some glasses.

- A linen sheet is perfect for a tablecloth. Wrap glasses in linen napkins so they don't break during the journey.

- Buy an Opinel pocketknife to use for all the picnics you will ever have anywhere – but preferably in Paris.

6

LE DÎNER

For many Parisians, the perfect restaurant is the bistro on the corner. It may not the height of class, but there's always an easy-going ambiance.

44,000 RESTAURANTS

When in Paris, where must I eat? This is usually the first question people ask me. Paris is the city with the largest number of cafés and restaurants in the world: no fewer than 160 per square kilometre! Still, this is not so surprising in itself. Unlike most other countries where going out for drinks or a meal is considered a luxury, in Paris it's been part of daily life from way back. There are various reasons for this. One is that many writers and artists used to work in cafés. In addition, eating lunch behind your desk at work was forbidden for years, and social life hardly ever takes place at home, but generally outdoors. Most people live in a small house, so there's limited space for having friends over. In addition, the classic Hausmannian buildings are extremely noisy. And considering that most Parisians have hardly any time to cook, but want to enjoy good food, it's not that surprising that Paris counts over 44,000 restaurants.

No particular one of these 44,000 restaurants is by definition 'best'. The simple but infinitely original vegetable dishes by Septime cannot be compared to a good old *steak au poivre* from Bistrot Paul Bert. The prohibitively expensive chocolate cake with caviar by Bruno Verjus – who may just be the best contemporary chef of the moment – is something you must try at least once in your life, but the same goes for the baos available at the Yam'Tcha tea shop for 4.50 euros. Fancy some *fruits de mer*? These seafood platters are easily available in a classic brasserie where champagne seems to flow in abundance, but also in a regular café. And starred restaurants are by no means the only places to go for the very best wines, because these days a *cave à manger* (a wine bar where food is served) will also do nicely.

In recent years, I have tried a wide range of locations for a meal. I've had breakfast at a fish shop where for years there has been one single table available for the lucky passer-by who happens to fancy half a dozen oysters. I've had lunch at a butcher who cooks the best entrecôtes in the city for you right there in the shop, and I've had meals prepared by famous starred chefs, as well dishes created by chefs from the new generation. The list goes on and on, because everywhere I go, I hear or read about yet another newly recommended address. Needless to say that after seven years my to-eat list is only expanding.

So, where to go? My best advice is to visit as many different types of restaurants as possible. Parisian restaurants can be roughly subdivided into five types, which, for the sake of convenience, I'll briefly explain below and continue discussing them in a little more depth later. Alternate a lunch at a brasserie with a meal at a neo-bistro, and after a visit to a starred restaurant, have a meal at a simple bouillon eatery. This will give you a good idea of Parisian gastronomy, which is infinite.

Bistros & neo-bistros
These are small-scale, friendly venues with tables close together. Maybe not the height of high-class dining, but they are ever so charming and easy-going. The walls of traditional bistros are generally entirely covered with photos and posters. They serve uncomplicated wine and simple classics, such as *blanquette de veau* or a homemade terrine. Combine the accessible atmosphere and low prices of a classic bistro with higher quality and voilà; there's your neo-bistro.

Brasseries
Brasseries are large-scale, impressive venues that feature high ceilings, numerous mirrors and impeccably dressed waiters. There's no better place to be seen than a brasserie, where champagne will flow abundantly and menus are extensive. They serve *choucroute, foie gras* and *fruits de mer*.

Bouillons
With classic dishes at very friendly prices, these restaurants have made a great comeback. It's worth noting that most of them are established in large and listed buildings. They generally do not allow advance booking, but the queues go faster than you might expect.

Starred restaurants
Paris has over one hundred starred restaurants, ten of which have been awarded three Michelin stars. In addition to the very famous names, there are plenty of young talents, including a significant number of Japanese chefs.

Caves à manger
In recent years, these wine bars where food is served have been on the up and up. Although their menus are generally limited to a few modest dishes, their wine list is far more extensive.

LE
BISTRO

The very first thing I put in the moving van seven years ago to take with me to Paris was my bike, under the assumption that it would be essential for my culinary exploratory expeditions. With it I would find the best croissants in the city, *brocantes* at unknown locations, the shops with the loveliest tableware and that particular cheese that is sold only under the counter… I was determined to discover, smell and taste everything. The main quest was, naturally, to find the very best restaurant in the city. As a result, my initial months in Paris constituted a jumble of bicycle routes. At considerable risk to my own life I might add, because cycling was almost exclusively restricted to bus lanes.

Since then, my bicycle has collected heaps of dust. This is by no means attributable to Paris, because in recent years kilometres of new bicycle

paths have been laid out and even my neighbours – yes, the same neighbours that would frown whenever I jumped on my bike for yet another exploratory expedition – now do their shopping *à velo*. In addition, the number of restaurants worth a detour has continued to increase. No, the issue was rather that I learned to eat like a Parisian.

No Parisian will ever contemplate walking for longer than ten minutes to get a baguette, crossing the river Seine for a cake or tart or taking *Le Metro* to have lunch in another district. Instead, they tend to live and remain in their very own neighbourhood. The *quartiers* resemble small villages where you find everything you might possibly need. So the issue at hand is not the best restaurant in the city, but the best restaurant in your neighbourhood.

Obviously, every Parisian has a different favourite restaurant, because – with few exceptions – it's usually the bistro on the corner. Everyone goes there: from a plumber to a lawyer and retired physician to upcoming artist. The food will seldom fail, provided you manage your expectations. They are not starred restaurants where you book a table weeks before and traverse half the city to get there. This is where you plop yourself into your chair after a hard day's work to enjoy a glass of wine and a *plat du jour*.

Their menus – if they have one at all – are generally no longer that a single side of paper. Usually there's a blackboard with simple, affordable daily meals. They won't serve lobster and caviar, but you will get sausages, *boeuf bourguignon, blanquette de veau* and *steak frites*; all prepared with copious amounts of butter.

There was a time when bistros were generally managed by married couples, with the husband working as the host and the wife as the chef. Although this has largely become a thing of the past, the atmosphere in many bistros is still very homey. Le patron is present without exception and invariably greets guests with a handshake, often even with a hug. No matter how busy things are, there is always room for regulars – an extra table can be set up if required. With tables close enough to one another to overhear conversations, you'll quickly make new acquaintances and learn what's going on in your neighbourhood. So these bistros provide a place to eat, and also function as a living room for the entire *quartier*.

PILATES SERVED WITH SAUSAGE

My favourite bistro dish is *saucisse purée*. It consists of a homemade sausage, a generous portion of mashed potatoes and plenty of gravy. In other words: comfort food the French way. Heavy? Oh, yes. Fortunately, in Paris this dish can now be combined with a new sport: *Pilates saucisse*. After booking, you do one hour of Pilates, followed by a glass of wine and a plate of food. These Pilates-and-sausage lessons were invented by my neighbour the culinary author Xavier Vankerrebrouck. Xavier has dedicated his life to sausage, wine and his second wife, a Pilates teacher. Says it all. If you haven't had enough exercise yet, you can join the Running Flan Club (@runningflanclub_) every Saturday morning. The idea is simple: run for a few kilometres, then have some flan – from a different pastry chef every time. It's a huge success, which is rather exceptional because Parisians usually limit physical activity to walking, doing yoga and engaging in the occasional love affair.

NEO-BISTROS

During the 1990s, many French chefs became tired of working in formal restaurants. They were fine with the high-level environment, but did not enjoy all the fuss that came with it. At the same time, the level of most bistros needed a boost and many people had had enough of having to spend a fortune on a meal. And this is how possibly the most important movement in recent restaurant history came about: the bistronomy – a contraction of the words bistro and gastronomy.

Pioneers such as Yves Camdeborde of Le Comptoir du Relais were so successful that long queues formed outside their businesses almost immediately. I don't go there anymore, but I honestly think they deserve a statue because they paved the way for an entire generation of neo-bistros, which

PILATES SAUCISSE

**Le samedi 4 juillet 11h
Square Louis XVI 8e**

**27€ : un cours, une saucisse purée
et un verre de vin**

in turn has resulted in an incredible improvement generally of the standard of the middle segment. They also made going out for a meal in the higher segment just so much more relaxed, in Paris as well as the rest of the world.

STARRED CHEFS & BISTROS

Famous starred chefs didn't hesitate to take the plunge and start their own bistros, the traditional type in particular. This has to do with their infinite respect for the classics: in Paris, the old school must be honoured at all costs. If an iconic venue finds itself in financial trouble, there will always be a chef prepared to take it over. Interiors and the essence of the cuisines will be maintained, but at a higher standard because they will use better products. Chefs such as Alain Ducasse and Jean François Piège now own a fair number of bistros, some of them really good. I like to eat at Ducasse's Aux Lyonnais. Piège has blown new life into the ancient À l'Epi d'Or, also definitely worth trying. The prices in these bistros tend to be somewhat higher and you'll see more tourists, but their food is usually excellent.

♀ THREE FAVOURITES

Les Arlots The best *saucisse purée* in Paris is served at this venue, owned by chef Thomas Brachet. *136 Rue du Faubourg Poissonnière, 10th*
Le Servan This neo-bistro is one of my favourite places for lunch. And they are open on Mondays too! *32 Rue Saint-Maur, 11th*
Bistrot Paul Bert This is where you get a high-quality *steak au poivre*, but I actually come for their fried eggs with truffle. *18 Rue Paul Bert, 11th*

❤ MUST-HAVE: BISTRO CHAIRS

My Paris apartment didn't come with a balcony, so I kept mine on the patio of my house in Amsterdam: my French bistro chairs. You'll see them at almost every Parisian outdoor café, usually red, dark blue, black or dark green, but feel free to compile your own colour combination.
www.maisonlouisdrucker.com

NO, PARISIAN WAITERS ARE NOT GRUMPY

- Parisian waiters, grumpy? *Mais non!* They do come with an instruction manual, however. Once you act accordingly, you are guaranteed a lovely evening.

- French waiters take their job seriously, and the principle of *égalité* possibly even more: everyone is equal. So always treat waiters with respect.

- Your entrance also matters and a simple *bonjour* won't do. In France, people greet each other using two words: *bonjour monsieur* or *bonjour madame*.

- Never address the waiter using the word *garçon* because it's considered disrespectful. Instead, call them *monsieur* or *madame* at all times.

- It's also not done to simply plop down when you arrive. Wait until the waiter sees you, greet him or her and indicate whether you have come for a drink or a meal. They will then point out a table to you.

- If you prefer to sit somewhere else, this is no problem at all – provided you have properly gone through the previous steps. Once you've made a good start, you'll find that French waiters are surprisingly flexible.

- Make eye contact and say *'s'il vous plaît'* if you need the waiter's attention. You might raise your hand, but not too high. And then: do not wave, do not call or shout and certainly refrain from clapping your hands or snapping your fingers.

- Only leave after you have said goodbye. Once you've done all the above, you will certainly be given a better table if you return.

LA BRASSERIE

When I first entered a large Parisian brasserie as a child, I was enchanted by its grandeur. The magnificent backdrop, the restrained yet chic clothes of the guests sipping their champagne, the waiters racing through the establishment carrying gigantic platters of oysters and lobsters. The crêpes that were flambéed with a grand gesture… It was really all a restaurant had to be. Ever since that first time, for me Paris is inextricably connected with brasseries such as La Coupole, Bofinger and Terminus Nord.

Brasseries are part of the legacy of the Franco-Prussian War that took place in the second half of the nineteenth century, when many French Alsatians fled the German occupation and established homes in Paris. Their beer halls came along with them. The French word brasserie is derived from the German word *brauhaus*, or 'brewery'. This also explains why their menus always include specialities from Alsace, such as sauerkraut dishes referred to as *choucroutes*.

The concept of the brasserie was an instant success. Famous Parisians loved to spend time in these establishments, from Sartre to Simone de Beauvoir and from Colette to Cocteau. This allowed brasseries such as La Coupole, Lipp and Bofinger to rapidly develop into city icons. Nonetheless, the heyday of the brasserie seems to be over because most of these Parisian icons now belong to the same owner and are packed with tourists.

But this certainly doesn't mean you should skirt around them. Plenty of locals still love to eat in these establishments, but they generally enjoy their meals at different times and tend to sit in other parts of the brasserie, which I will discuss in greater detail below. I regularly go to a brasserie, which undoubtedly has to do with my sense of nostalgia. Time seems to have stopped in brasseries: very little ever changes in them, let alone their menus. It's as comforting as it is reassuring.

When I took my son to Bofinger for the first time, I recognised the enchantment in his eyes that I had experienced during my first visit. The admiration for those impeccably dressed waiters, that feeling of doubt when tasting your very first oyster and the craving for those profiteroles on the next table.

With a bit of luck, history will repeat itself and someday my son will introduce his children to a Parisian brasserie. The lamb curry will still be on the menu at La Coupole. Table 8 will still be the most wanted table at Lipp, and the *choucroute* by Bofinger will taste exactly the same. When he orders their very first oysters, he will recognise the look of enchantment in their eyes. In other words: if all goes well, my memories will one day be his, thanks to the brasserie.

THE BEST PLACE TO SIT

Lipp
According to a Parisian urban legend, Lipp is divided into heaven, purgatory and the inferno of hell. Those who are pointed to a table on the first floor might as well immediately leave the scene, because this is the hell of Paris, predestined for tourists. A better place is in purgatory; the part in the area to the back of the ground floor. The front section of the ground floor – heaven – is reserved for the *belle clientèle*. Tables 1 through 8 are even considered paradise. *151 Boulevard Saint-Germain, 6th*

Bofinger
Each hall in this iconic brasserie is as breath-taking as the next, but the tables under the leaded dome are definitely the most sought-after. The one everyone wants is table 11, which has the best view. *5-7 Rue de la Bastille, 4th*

Terminus Nord
Still one of the best classic Paris brasseries is Terminus Nord, with those magic restaurant noises you only hear in busy brasseries – just close your eyes and listen to the clinking of glasses, the humming voices of other customers, the clattering of cutlery… no music could ever beat this. Best tables are numbers 710 and number 712. *23 Rue de Dunkerque, 10th*

La Coupole
This Art Deco brasserie was once the favourite of Sartre, Man Ray and Josephine Baker. It's still a great place to be, as long as you get a good table. Those around the iconic sculpture of Louis Derbré are most popular by far. Table 22 is considered the best, but I prefer table 23. *102 Boulevard du Montparnasse, 14th*

Au Pied de Cochon
This brasserie near Les Halles is open 24 hours a day, seven days a week. So if you ever wake up at 7 am and fancy some onion soup or a few oysters after a wild night on the town, this is the place to go. Table 130 is my favourite. *6 Rue Coquillière, 1st*

VISIT A BRASSERIE LIKE A PARISIAN

- The French tend to eat late in the evening, so if you are planning to visit a popular brasserie and would rather avoid the tourist masses, be sure to book a table for the second shift, at around 9 pm. Families with whining children will have retreated to their hotels by then.

- Most brasseries feature a long sofa on one side of the table and a chair on the other. It's an unwritten rule that women take a seat on the sofa and men on the chair: this way, the woman is faced towards the room to be admired, while the man will only have eyes for her.

- Manage your culinary expectations: some brasseries are visited mainly to enjoy the atmosphere. As a French colleague once wrote about the iconic Lipp: 'When you come to eat here, just bring your inner poet and leave your inner restaurant critic at home'.

- If you want good food, you can never go wrong by ordering *fruits de mer* or a classic such as *choucroute*.

- There's no place in the world where the location of a table is of greater importance than in a Paris brasserie. After all, it's all about seeing and being seen. More often than not, the tables at the centre are considered the best, because from there you can see who enters and who leaves. So, when booking a table, indicate your chosen table. If you are unhappy with it, ask whether you can wait for another one at the bar. A common trick is to order a glass of champagne while waiting as a sign that you intend to spend some serious money.

FRUITS DE MER

In Paris, you see *fruits de mer* everywhere you turn. In principle, you can order them right through the year, but the best time is from October through January. The best venues to go for a substantial seafood platter are the large brasseries – in beautiful clothes and seated at a perfectly set table with a bottle of champagne… this is about as good as it gets in Paris, or so I used to think, anyway. My years in Paris have taught me that *fruits de mer* can also be a simple street food, served in markets on a plastic plate. Some fish shops have a few tables where you can eat on the spot, such as at La Marée Beauvau at the Marché d'Aligre. Some Paris cafés serve it as well, particularly oysters.

The best example is found in the 12th arrondissement at Le Baron Rouge, frequented by a rather odd blend of market vendors, chic French people and tourists. You'll find most of the customers drunk, irrespective of the time of day. I like to go there during the oyster season, when on Saturdays and Sundays the oyster sellers set up outside. Order a bottle of wine and – for form's sake – a carafe of water inside and the oysters outside, where they are opened on the spot. But be warned: chances are slim that you'll leave the place sober.

HOW TO EAT AN OYSTER

Contrary to many other countries, in Paris oysters are not cut from their shell. This may be construed as sloppy service, but naturally it has everything to do with taste: the French are convinced that this will keep the oysters fresher for a longer period of time. It's up to you to cut the adductor muscle using the side of the oyster fork. Be careful though: connoisseurs swear that the attachment is the best part of the oyster, so don't miss out on this.

You should know that the shell includes two different types of fluid: sea water and nectar. When you open an oyster, the sea water usually flows out immediately. When oysters are being prepared, this fluid is drained away. The fluid the oyster secretes two minutes after opening is not sea water, but nectar. Nectar is rich in minerals and flavour, so be sure to drink it. During a formal dinner, bring oysters to your mouth using an oyster fork before putting the shell to your lips to drink the fluid.

About the flavourings served with oysters: before you start using them, taste a pure oyster to decide whether it needs any additions. I sometimes use a pinch of pepper, but I prefer to eat them pure. And last but not least: don't swallow an oyster all at once, but chew a few times so the flavours are released.

♀ THREE FAVOURITES

Bofinger The place to go for an impressive platter of *fruits de mer* in an equally impressive brasserie. *5-7 Rue de la Bastille, 4th*
Clamato A much more accessible venue, which for years has been one of my favourite places to go. They serve delicious shellfish. *80 Rue de Charonne, 11th*
Le Baron Rouge This is where – during weekends only – you can enjoy oysters in a café. *1 Rue Théophile Roussel, 12th*

A CRASH COURSE IN OYSTERS

- The French word for oyster is *huître*. They are generally ordered by the *douzaine* or *demi-douzaine*; twelve or six.

- Oysters are opened by an *écailler*; an oyster seller who opens oysters at record speed.

- For oysters, a distinction is made between *plates* and *creuses*: flat and hollow.

- *Spéciales* are usually somewhat larger and fleshier than *fines*. *Papillons* are very small specimens.

- In France, the size of oysters is generally indicated using a number. *Creuses* receive the number 00-6. The higher the number, the smaller the oyster, so the number 00 indicates the largest ones available.

- In Paris, oysters are served with *mignonette*, a red wine vinegar-based sauce with finely chopped shallot.

LE BOUILLON

If you have little time and money, bouillons – traditional French eateries – are the place to go. Often located in magnificent buildings, they were invented in the mid-nineteenth century by Paris butcher Pierre Louis Duval. He came up with the idea to provide market workers and traders of the fresh products market in Les Halles with a healthy and affordable meal. Most of them lived far from the city centre and did not have the opportunity to go home for lunch. An additional benefit was that he could market his unsold meat. He opened his first bouillon in 1854 in the Rue de la Monnaie. The menu included veal stew, leg of lamb and naturally: *bouillon* (broth), known to be nutritious and easy to digest. It's an understatement to say that the concept caught on. Around 1900, when bouillons were at their peak, Paris counted about 250 of them. This made it the ultimate fast food restaurant during the Belle Époque. Their success didn't last though: due to industrialisation and the advance

of the *nouveau riche*, most bouillons were ousted by fancy brasseries. One bouillon succeeded in keeping its doors open: Chartier, a legendary venue at the Rue du Faubourg Montmartre that has been an uninterrupted resounding success. It has 280 seats and an average of 1,500 guests a day. I am in the habit of taking friends who come to visit Paris for the first time to Chartier. Not because of the quality of the food as such – this is actually far from perfect – but because of the characteristic waiters who will scribble your order on the paper tablecloth, their rapid service and its design inspired by a classic station hall. Dismissing Chartier as a tourist trap does not do it justice, as even the snobbiest of Parisians praise its ambiance.

Meanwhile, Parisian bouillons are experiencing a comeback. In recent years, a substantial number of them have opened their doors, often in buildings that used to accommodate chic brasseries. This renewed popularity is easily explained by the huge concerns about purchasing power in France, the rising prices charged at hotels and restaurants and the increasing demand for affordable eateries, in Paris in particular. Bouillon opening hours are another factor to be taken into account. They open at noon and close late in the evening; convenient for families with young children as well as millennials who are no longer bothered by traditional mealtimes.

And then there is their menu, which is virtually identical in each bouillon and excels in simplicity, unpretentiousness and recognisability. And as it goes, the more instability there is in the world, the greater the need for certainty and reassurance on your plate. Bouillon menus are perfectly in line with this sentiment. You will not come across any insignificant sides here, but instead straightforward dishes well-known to all French citizens. Onion soup, *escargots* or leek in vinaigrette as an appetiser, while main courses still involve meat and poultry: *blanquette de veau, boeuf bourguignon* or *saucisse purée*. Desserts such as *chou chantilly, profiteroles* or *riz au lait* are also old-time favourites.

PLEASE JOIN THE QUEUE

Most bouillons do not provide options for booking, so there's no need to plan your visit beforehand. You sometimes have to wait in line, but those queues move on faster than you might think. The staff inside keep things going at a brisk pace and guests are expected to leave right after they have finished eating, instead of lingering. Order, eat, pay and split: that's the idea.

♀ THREE FAVOURITES

Bouillon Chartier Evening after evening, the immaculately dressed waiters make for an enjoyable spectacle. *7 Rue du Faubourg Montmartre, 9th*
Bouillon Julien You will see flowers, peacocks and nymphs everywhere you look in this Art Nouveau temple. *16 Rue du Faubourg Saint-Denis, 10th*
Bouillon Pigalle This bouillon has the best kitchen of all. Don't miss out on their *œufs mayonnaise* and *baba au rum*. *22 Boulevard de Clichy, 18th*

LET'S TALK MONEY

- Paris is expensive? Not necessarily. A *menu du jour* is far less expensive than eating à la carte. A brasserie such as Bofinger, for instance, charges 19 euros for its lunch menu; an à la carte meal will easily cost three times the amount.

- At good restaurants, lunches are more affordable than dinners anyway because lunch menus are more modest. You may also find that à la carte prices are sometimes lower during the day. At Le Grand Colbert, oysters are more expensive in the evening than in the afternoon.

- Order a *carafe d'eau* instead of *eau mineral*. You will be brought a carafe of tap water, which in Paris is always free of charge.

- Choose your addresses carefully and consider that you are also paying for the location. Would you consider 16 euros to be a substantial price to pay for a mediocre cup of coffee in the Ritz? Certainly. But bear in mind that it is served at a historic spot you'll always remember.

- The same applies to restaurants. Every time you visit Paris, choose one really good restaurant that is on your bucket list.

- In France, service charges are usually included in the price, which explains why Parisians are far less generous tippers than you'd expect; it's a gesture rather than an obligation. Nonetheless, about 5 to 10 per cent tips are given in the better restaurants without many exceptions.

OLD AND NEW STARS

Paris features over one hundred starred restaurants, each one distinctive. Prices at three-star venues are much higher than at top restaurants in other European cities, so be sure to research them before heading out. Decide whether you'd like to eat at a famous restaurant from the old generation or at a restaurant with an emerging talent. I myself once started with The Great Three as described below. After all, where would you be without the timeless classics? Then again, this is by no means to say that you wouldn't enjoy a better meal at an establishment run by the new generation.

THE GREAT THREE

Alain Passard
When in 2001 this French top chef said that he was going to remove meat and fish from his menu, the entire culinary scene was in uproar. Dinner at a three-star restaurant without lobster, caviar or *foie gras*? Unthinkable in those days, in Paris in particular. Vegetarians cheered, and many gourmands expressed horror, but everyone was keen to eat at his restaurant l'Arpège. So was I. I was still in my student days and because a meal at Passard cost about one month's study grant, his beetroot cooked in salt crust became one of my most memorable birthday gifts ever. What Passard did was pioneering, because in those days restaurants used vegetables as little more than a garnish. He was one of the first chefs to show that

gastronomy was not just about the most expensive turbot and largest truffle, but about the most beautiful tomatoes and tastiest French beans. Passard quickly became a hero to countless chefs. Now, a new generation has emerged that may be even better with vegetables than he is. For fans, however, Passard's restaurant l'Arpège will always be a place of pilgrimage. *84 Rue de Varenne, 7th*

Pierre Gagnaire
Pierre Gagnaire is the ultimate hero of Sergio Herman and countless other chefs. Son of a chef, he enjoyed a classical education and learned the trade at Paul Bocuse and other establishments, but soon emerged as one of the most creative chefs in the history of French gastronomy. Today, Gagnaire owns restaurants all over the world – some of them in Paris – with over 14 Michelin stars in total. Known for his sense of aesthetics, he was one of the great innovators of his generation. A visit to his three-star establishment at the Rue Balzac is costly, but don't let that hold you back.
6 Rue Balzac, 8th

Alain Ducasse
In 1984, a plane in which Alain Ducasse was a passenger crashed during a storm in the Alps. All of the passengers died, except Ducasse, then a young chef. Naturally this was a turning point in his life. As a student of culinary greats such as Michel Guérard and Roger Vergé, Ducasse had already proved himself to be extremely ambitious. After the accident, however, his perfectionism took on Herculean qualities. When, in 1987, Ducasse was hired to raise the status of the restaurant of the prestigious hotel Le Louis XV in Monaco to a higher plane, he insisted on stipulating in his contract that he could be fired if he failed to scoop three Michelin stars within four years. The unimaginable happened: he bagged the third star within three years. It proved to be just the start of an ever-expanding gastronomic empire. Ducasse is one of the greatest chefs on earth and a cookery book author slash master slash chocolate guru. He owns over twenty restaurants worldwide and an impressive number of Michelin stars. I once had a meal at his three-star restaurant in Paris, but I must admit that nowadays I would rather go to Aux Lyonnais, his bouchon in the 2nd arrondissement.

JAPANESE MASTERS

The most interesting current movement by far is the new generation of Japanese chefs. This is not really all that surprising: traditionally, Japanese and French chefs admire and respect each other very much. Their cuisines, as refined and product-oriented as they are, adhere to a strict relationship between master and pupil. The fusion is also recognised by the large number of top French restaurants in Tokyo and the numerous Japanese addresses in Paris. In recent years, many Japanese chefs have started working for great French masters, which has resulted in a new generation of emerging Japanese chefs who combine the best of both worlds. They have succeeded in creating an extremely pure, light and tremendously interesting version of French cuisine, the best example of which is Kei Kobayashi. With a classic Japanese chef as a father, he learned the trade from French top chefs such as Alain Ducasse. Today Kobayashi has his very own establishment characterised by an entirely personal French-Japanese signature. He is also the first Japanese chef in France to be awarded a third Michelin star. His bread filled with chestnuts and honey is a treat I'll never forget. **Kei** *5 Rue Coq Héron, 1st*

VEGETABLE KINGS

Thanks to Alain Passard, Parisian restaurants now use vegetables much more than they did before, especially among a new generation of chefs. Septime is perhaps the best example of this development. In this light-filled establishment, vegetables often play a leading part, leaving meat and fish to play a minor role as flavourings. I once had a roasted tomato with a chicken broth-based sauce. Despite having just one Michelin star, Septime has been included on the list of best restaurants in the world for many years. So how do you get yourself a booking for one of those coveted tables? I'll let you in on the secret in a bit. **Septime** *80 Rue de Charonne, 11th*

CHINESE STARS

Chef Adeline Grattard of Yam'Tcha combines Chinese and French cuisine with an elegant and original style of cooking. And while I am normally not the first to recommend refraining from enjoying a lovely glass of wine with your lunch in Paris, I am happy to make an exception here. For each course, Adeline's husband Chi Wah Chan pours a different extraordinary tea he brings especially from China. They serve a set menu which is so cleverly constructed that, after six courses, you will leave feeling recharged and full of energy, ready to explore more of Paris. If you don't succeed in booking a table, you should know that they sell the best teas and baos available at their teashop in the Rue Sauval. **Yam'Tcha** *121 Rue Saint-Honoré, 2nd*

♀ THREE MORE FAVOURITES

Maison Sota One of the city's most beautiful restaurants; and also one of the most interesting, thanks to Sota Atsumi's culinary art. *3 Saint Hubert, 11th*
Table Book your table at the bar, from where you can see the kitchen. Do try their chocolate cake with caviar. *3 Rue de Prague, 12th*
Mosuke Chef Mory Sacko is known for his marvellous blend of African and French cuisine. *11 Rue Raymond-Losserand, 14th*

HOW TO GET
THE MOST WANTED TABLES

- Some restaurants seem to be fully booked all the time. If you do want to get a table, start by checking how their booking system works. At Septime, for instance, tables can be booked for a maximum of three weeks in advance. So if you want to book a table on 23 March, be ready to book a table online on 2 March.

- If this fails, you could send an e-mail to the restaurant asking whether they can put you on the waiting list. I always do this a few days before and succeed in getting a table nine times out of ten.

- Another idea is to come by a day before and ask them to call you should someone unexpectedly cancel their table.

- Regulars usually take priority: often, you can book a table for your next visit when paying.

- An increasing number of restaurants no longer have the option of booking a table, which reinforces the neighbourhood function. Check their opening times and go there either shortly before they open or a little later after the first shift is done.

- If you haven't been able to book a table anywhere, go to a brasserie or bouillon, most of which are open seven days a week. You can usually wait for a table outside or at the bar.

LA CAVE
À MANGER

Should you now be under the illusion that I spend every minute in Paris in restaurants, you are very much mistaken. If I have enjoyed an extensive lunch, I really don't feel like lingering over a long meal in the evening, especially if I need to get up early the next morning. In such cases, a *cave à manger* – which are becoming increasingly popular – comes in very handy. They are actually licensed wine shops. The licenses are granted only if they serve food, so in addition to a very extensive selection of wines, most caves also feature a limited menu. Some of them consist of a mere two or three small dishes, along with some charcuterie, cheeses and bread. But all of the best possible quality, making them perfect venues for an *apéro* or modest meal. Another great advantage is that you can take home that bottle of wine you particularly like. The new generation of *caves* often serves natural wines. Also good to know: *caves à manger* do not provide the option of booking. Impractical? Maybe, but it does ensure they remain lively venues with an important neighbourhood function. You'll thus find most *caves* packed with Parisians, either at a table or standing. If you want to make sure you have a table, the best thing to do is check their opening hours and be on the doorstep when they open.

♥ THREE FAVOURITES

Billili One of the liveliest, fun and delicious places in Paris. Their *tarama* is highly recommended. *136 Rue du Faubourg Poissonnière, 10th*

Poney Club Top-quality natural wines served with charcuterie, cheeses and bread of the same high standard. *Rue Eugene Carrière, 18th*

La Buvette A tiny establishment in a former cheese shop. Try their broad beans with lemon. *67 Rue Saint-Maur, 11th*

WHAT TO WEAR WHEN GOING TO A RESTAURANT?

- There's basically just one thing to remember: in Paris, it's better to be underdressed than overdressed.

- Never wear an outfit that seems to be too well-considered. Parisians take pride in looking like they casually threw something on. Don't overdo your accessories either; choose one piece of jewellery, a good shawl and a leather or clutch bag.

- Keep it modest. Black, white and dark blue are timeless. A white shirt or a tuxedo jacket and jeans will always do the trick.

- Choose natural fabrics, such as cotton, silk, linen or wool. Wear clothing that's a size too big instead of too small.

- Never wear anything with a logo on it: in Paris, this is considered cheap. A logo on a handbag or clutch bag remains just within allowable limits.

- Don't wear too much make-up. Many Parisian women wear just a little bit of mascara.

- Don't show too much skin. You seldom see a man wearing shorts in Paris. Women may wear clothing that leaves either the legs or arms uncovered, preferably not both.

- As regards shoes: black loafers will always do. Sneakers are fine when going to a bistro or wine bar, preferably Reebok, Adidas or Nike and certainly not from one of the main fashion houses. Heels? Sure, but only if you can walk on them perfectly.

THE NEW PARIS

Before I came to live in Paris, to me the city consisted mainly of clichés. Delightful and exquisite clichés, but still, clichés. A weekend in Paris involved breakfast at Hotel Costes, lunch at Café de Flore, aperitifs at Palette in the Rue du Seine, *fruits de mer* at Terminus Nord, cocktails in the Marais and browsing the shops at old and familiar Saint Germain. Because there was absolutely no way I could afford a house in Saint Germain, seven years ago I came to live in Pigalle at the foot of Montmartre in a neighbourhood where sex workers and musicians used to live. This was an entirely different side of Paris, teeming with neo-bistros, bars selling natural wines, eateries and young talents. Since then, I have alternated between the old and the new Paris. Because no matter how addicted I have become to all of those iconic venues, in Paris gastronomy involves just so much more than the great classics and also, much more than French cuisine.

Parisian restaurants and supermarkets clearly show that it is a melting pot of cultures. Lebanese tabouleh is sold on virtually every street corner. And in addition to countless *jambon-beurres, bánh mì* are also in high demand for lunch. You'll find great noodle bars throughout the city, and every neighbourhood supermarket sells Greek *tarama*. I could go on forever. Each of these gastronomic cultures really deserves its own book, but for now let me give you a quick crash course.

♀ THREE FAVOURITES

The Hood Asian street food is served here all day. Don't miss the chance to try their kaya toast for brunch. *80 Rue Jean-Pierre Timbaud, 11ᵗʰ*
Chez Bob de Tunis The Tunisian sandwiches prepared at Bob's are iconic. *10 Rue Richer, 9ᵗʰ*
Ama Siam I just love this colourful and younger version of famous Lao restaurant Lao Siam. *49 Rue de Belleville, 19ᵗʰ*

A CRASH COURSE IN THE NEW PARIS

- Paris features not one, but two, China Towns. The first is located south of the Rue de Tolbiac in the 13th arrondissement; the second in Belleville in the 20th.

- The French have a particularly soft spot for Greek cuisine. Paris is brimming with high-quality Greek caterers and delicatessens and has a rapidly growing number of trendy Greek bistros. I am particularly fond of Etsi in the 18th.

- Vietnam was once a French colony, so you'll find plenty of Vietnamese restaurants. Readily available throughout the city, the *bánh mì* by the Coupi Bar on Avenue de la Porte d'Ivry just might be the best.

- Fans of India go to Little Jaffna, the Indian district between Gare du Nord and Gare de l'Est. Make sure to check out the Passage Brady, where you'll find dozens of Indian restaurants and shops.

- If like me you are crazy about Japan, you should really be in and around the Rue Saint-Anne in the 2nd arrondissement which teems with Japanese eateries, noodle bars and supermarkets.

- From Lebanese ice cream to *labneh*: the love of Lebanon is seen in all of Paris. If you'd like to try lots of different flavours at the same time, you really should try Kubri in the 11th.

- African cuisines are also experiencing a moment. Actually that's putting it mildly, because for the last two years not a single table has been available at top chef Mory Sacko's restaurant Mosuke.

7

PARIS À LA MAISON

When Parisians cook at home, they rarely prepare a complete menu. Given the fact that Parisian kitchens are generally tiny, this comes as no surprise.

COOKING CONSTITUTES BUYING

If you want to enjoy a meal at home like Parisians do, there is absolutely no need to be a great chef. On the contrary, there's barely any need to even enter the kitchen. After all, gastronomy is not necessarily about spending hours hovering over pots and pans, it's about good food. And this is readily available in the many shops and delicatessens. So it's better to serve a *pot au feu* from your favourite caterer on a finely set table than a so-so dish, the time and effort of which you spent preparing has left you exhausted by the time your guests arrive. Buy the best cake or tart for dessert or compile your own cheese platter. Ensure it looks splendid, because presentation is everything, certainly in Paris.

POULET RÔTI

When Parisians cook at home, they rarely prepare a complete menu. This is not very surprising in view of their generally tiny kitchens and the perpetual rush almost everybody seems to be in. This does not alter

the fact that the average Parisian looks down their nose at microwave meals. The perfect solution is *poulet rôti*. You'll find these roasted chickens everywhere in Paris; at poulterers, markets, and most supermarkets. I have tried quite a few and have bought an especially good one from Parisian poulterer Atelier Gallus in the seventeenth. Their chickens are packaged in beautiful blue boxes imprinted with golden yellow letters. Children get homemade ketchup with it. Their secret? They first marinate the chicken in balsamic vinegar and *fleur de sel*. Shortly before roasting, the meat is massaged with a blend of clarified butter, herbs and garlic. Now that I think about it: a butter massage like this seems a golden opportunity for a massage parlour, but that's an altogether different topic.
Atelier Gallus, *14 Rue Saussier-Leroy, 17th*

PATÉ EN CROÛTE

Pâté en croute: yet another perfect option for a festive table that doesn't involve any trouble or effort whatsoever. A common French dish for centuries, preparing this fancy pâté in a pastry crust is a time-consuming task. Originally the golden brown and often richly adorned crust was intended only for cooking and preserving the pâté, but today it's eaten. The French love the combination of the golden brown crust and refined pâté in thick jelly and consume about 6.5 million kilos of *pâté en croûte* every year. Pâtés generally have a pork or veal base, but they come in many varieties: from chicken to rabbit and quail to duck liver. Ingredients always involve additional flavours, such as nuts or apples, plums, olives or truffles. The Dordogne has a pâté with woodcock, while in Amiens they make it with duck and rennet apples. The flavours of a *pâté en croute* are much more refined than that of a terrine. I once came across a vegetarian variant in Paris, made with tomato, courgette, aubergine and cumin.

Pâté en croûte should be served at room temperature so the jelly softens slightly, bringing out the distinctive flavours. I think it doesn't need any garnish at all, but serve it with a fresh sour green salad for a perfect meal instead of a fancy starter. I often take it abroad with me, at Christmas for instance.

Yohan Lastre sells a really outstanding *pâté en croute*. His shop just might be my all-time favourite in Paris: I have never seen so much craftsmanship combined with skill contained in so few square metres. The first time I went there, the shop window was displaying a giant pig's head made from *rillettes*. Once inside, you'll find an extremely small but fine selection of the most beautiful and original pâtés in Paris – or indeed in all of France. Maison Verot is a good alternative. Similar to many fashion houses, Verot has summer and winter collections. In addition to their phenomenal *pâtés en croûte* – I think the one with duck and figs is best – they have a wide selection of other classics. *Jambon persillé, andouillette, rillons* are all available here. **Lastre Sans Apostrophe**, *188 Rue de Grenelle, 7th* & **Maison Verot**, *38 Rue de Bretagne, 3rd*

RECIPE

CONFIT DE CANARD

Are you planning to cook a homemade meal but are in just as much of a rush as the average Parisian resident, then a can of *confit de canard* from your pantry is perfect. It will allow you to have dinner ready in half an hour. And your version would not be out of place in any bistro.

—————————— PREPARATION ——————————

Preheat the oven to 200 °C; I always use the grill.

Put the unopened can in warm water for ten minutes. This will allow the fat to melt and makes it easier to remove the duck from the can. Place the duck under the grill for 20 minutes.

Use the duck fat that's left in the can to pan-fry potatoes and serve them with the duck.

À EMPORTER

Choices are by no means limited to roast chicken, *confit de canard* and *pâté en croûte*. In Paris, you can buy entire platters of *fruits de mer* to take home, which many do around Christmas and New Year's Eve. Actually, over half of all the oysters consumed in a single year are eaten in the last two weeks of December. Some brasseries sell *plateaux à emporter* – to take away. Fish shops are also very happy to put together an immaculate platter for customers to take home.

It's a common sight on New Year's Eve: huge numbers of Parisians walking home carrying gigantic platters of *fruits de mer* to enjoy with family and friends. This also explains why in Paris the streets are so much quieter around New Year's Eve compared to other metropolises: most people are at home indulging in crab, langoustine and oysters. When I celebrate New Year's Eve in Paris, I always order the largest possible platter from my fish shop at the Rue des Martyrs. One bottle of good champagne to go with it *et voilà*.

UNE SALADE VERTE

Not everything can be bought or sold; not even in Paris. If there's one thing every home chef really should be able to prepare, it's a green salad with vinaigrette. You should know that the French generally don't eat their salad with their meal, but rather after the main course and before or with the cheese course afterwards. It is believed that a fresh salad cleanses the taste buds and benefits digestion.

When you visit a market, you immediately see how fond the French are of their salad leaves. The Friday Place d'Anvers market – one of my favourites – features an entire stand that exclusively sells varieties of lettuce. Granted, this may come across as slightly exaggerated, but never use pre-packaged lettuce, because it has no taste whatsoever. Simply buy a head of organic lettuce and rinse it at home. This also means that you simply can't do without the kitchen tool I use the most frequently: the salad spinner. In France, they're available at almost every supermarket.

Then there's this: lettuce leaves are delicate so tear them instead of slicing them. During dinner, gently pick up the leaves with your fork, possibly also with the help of your knife or a piece of bread.

VINAIGRETTE

SERVES 2-4

1 generous teaspoon of Dijon mustard
2 tablespoons of wine vinegar
Salt and pepper
100 ml of the best olive oil you can find

PREPARATION

Take a large salad bowl or mixing bowl – preferably the bowl you will be using to serve the salad. Add the mustard, vinegar and some salt and pepper and stir well into a homogenous mix. Add the oil drop by drop and keep stirring. Add some more oil if the vinaigrette is too thin. Taste again and add more mustard, vinegar or lemon juice if required. It's okay if the vinaigrette is quite sharp and sour. Arrange the rinsed and dried lettuce leaves on the vinaigrette, but do not mix until just before serving.

❤ MUST-HAVE: COPPER PANS

You really don't need high-end appliances or giant stoves to cook a good meal. Nobody in Paris has them, simply because the space in their kitchen doesn't allow for it. It's a far better idea to invest in a proper set of knives, a good chopping board and a few high-quality pans. I am really fond of the copper pans by Mauviel. They'll cost you dearly, but there really are no pans that conduct heat better. In addition to their stunning beauty, they are indestructible and therefore potential heirlooms. Which brings me to my excuse for buying them: they're not for me, they're for my son. The world-famous kitchen shop E. Dehillerin has them in a variety of types and sizes. *18-20 Rue Coquillière, 1st*

HOW TO HOST A PARISIAN DINNER

- Forget about starters and focus on the aperitif and main course.

- Buy a bottle of good champagne or another sparkling wine and put out a platter with some charcuterie and crudités. A good alternative is a platter of oysters.

- Serve the main course following the aperitif. Preferably choose a dish you are good at and which cooks without requiring your inspection or attention, such as a *coq au vin* or *boeuf bourguignon*. This will allow you to spend all your time on your guests. If this is too much fuss, simply buy a roasted chicken.

- Serve simple side dishes accompanied with some baguette and seasonal vegetables or a salad.

- After the meal, serve camembert or another cheese variety. An entire platter is often overdoing things. One cheese will do, as long as it's perfectly matured.

- Fancy something sweet? Go out and buy some exquisite chocolate at a chocolatier or some tasty ice cream from a good *glacier*.

- Don't fuss about wine. A cooled red wine will usually do, certainly if you're having Parisians over.

- You should be aware that Parisians are generally about a quarter of an hour late. This is considered polite in France, because it allows your host a little extra time.

TABLEWARE ADDICT

My dream house in Paris involved a kitchen jam-packed with copper pans, where every evening I would set the table with vintage linen. My cabinets would bulge with the tableware I had carefully assembled and collected at *brocantes* in the city. The reality, however, is not that romantic. It showed me that I had underestimated the price of copper pans, so the number of these pans I currently own is just five. My first home was too small to receive any guests, so covering the table with vintage linen made little sense. And during my first years in Paris, I didn't have any time to visit flea markets. So I simply bought some plates at Bouillon Chartier (which are actually quite nice and are available in their small shop on the Rue du Faubourg Montmartre) and that was it. It didn't matter, because I couldn't have fitted much more in my teeny-tiny kitchen anyway.

That dreamt-of tableware came later, when I had some time to spend searching. My new house came with a huge built-in china cabinet. It's full to bursting because Paris is synonymous with beautiful vintage tableware.

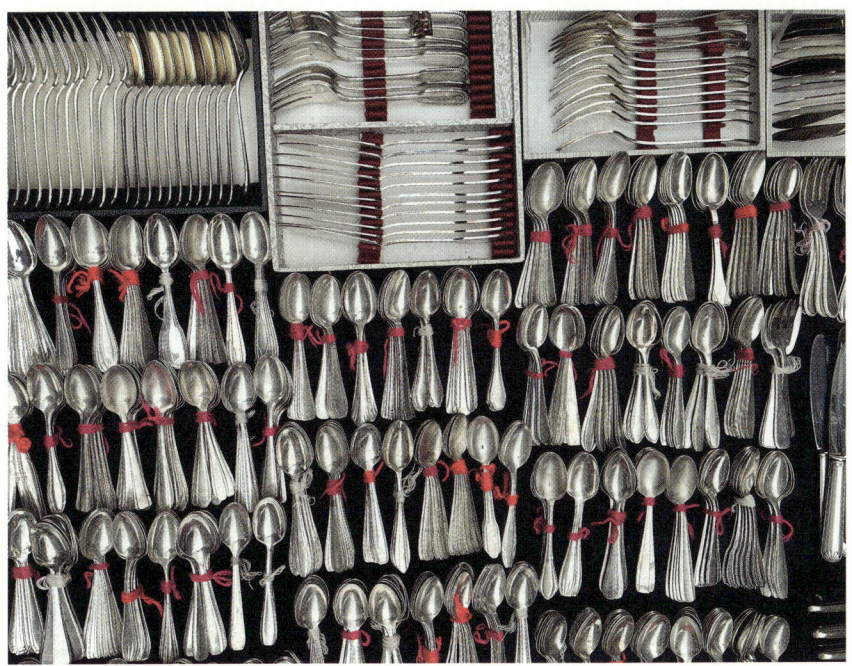

Paris is home to plenty of awesome shops, but I buy most of my things at *brocantes* and *vide greniers*. The French do not believe in throwing anything away, and by that, I mean literally *anything*. Since time immemorial, offal is used in dishes and white sneakers are without exception down-at-heel and seldom white. A sweater with a hole? Nobody will find fault with it in Paris – provided it's cashmere. The same goes for tableware. It's never thrown out, but instead sold. Which is great, because in Paris you can find plates for almost anything. From oyster plates to dishes for serving asparagus and artichoke plates… You can shop for crockery until you drop.

BROCANTES

The very best tableware to buy is vintage. At weekends, *brocantes* are held throughout Paris. Some take place on a weekly basis, such as the famous Marché au Puces de St-Ouen, which comprises eleven different markets, each with their own speciality. You'll find various restaurants as well, so you can easily spend an entire afternoon here. I have bought most of my finds at *brocantes* in the city centre. There are markets every weekend, often at unexpected locations. Go to *www.brocabrac.fr/75* to find out exactly where and when they are held while in Paris. Do note the difference between a *brocante* and a *vide grenier*. The latter translates into 'empty attic'. If you go to one, you really do have to go through the trouble of searching out nice plates and bowls among piles of rubbish. I'm quite a fan of this, but if you don't have much time and need an entire crockery service, a *brocante* or one of the shops below are better options.

♀ THREE FAVOURITES

Au Bain Marie A lovely address for silverware and antique oyster plates. *59 Bd Raspail, 6th*
AXS Design A true paradise filled with old plates. I once found some stunning oyster forks here. *12 rue Saint Sabin, 11th*
Merci If you prefer new tableware, you really have to check out this classic shop where I always buy my table linen. *111 Boulevard Beaumarchais, 3rd*

♥ MUST-HAVE: TABLEWARE FROM YOUR FAVOURITE RESTAURANT

I simply can't get enough of the tableware from Parisian brasseries and cafés. I have collected countless plates from Café de Flore, Bouillon Chartier and Brasserie Lipp. If it doesn't fit in your suitcase, simply order it at *www.giftshop.club* where you can find plenty of tableware from iconic Parisian addresses.

♥ MUST-HAVE:
CERAMICS BY ASTIER DE VILLATTE

The most beautiful ceramics you'll find in Paris are undoubtedly by Astier de Villatte. They are made from clay retrieved from the bottom of the river Seine. In addition to their plates and bowls, they also sell stunning kitchen light fixtures, such as their lamp inspired by a breadbasket. *173 Rue Saint-Honoré, 1st*

TIPS FOR A PARISIAN TABLE

- A well-set Parisian table is like a wardrobe: a mix of timeless pieces, vintage finds and, if possible, heirlooms. These don't have to be silver carafes; after all, heirlooms are all about the story.

- Make sure you have plenty of nice plates and serving dishes. You don't need a complete set. Quite the contrary, because everything the same often makes for a stiff and overly formal table. This doesn't mean you want a messy table. If you like things that tiny bit more formal, you might set it using lots of different plates in the same colour.

- Never skimp on good wine glasses. Use crystal glasses with a large bowl. Avoid coloured glassware.

- Don't save your best tableware for Christmas but set your table and use it on a regular Monday. After all, what's the use of crockery if it sees the light of day just once a year?

- Don't put plastic bottles on the table. Instead, buy a vintage water carafe.

- Linen tablecloths are very common in Paris. If you don't have one, you can use a linen bed sheet.

- Invest in high-quality napkins. Vintage napkins with embroidered initials can often be found at one of the many *brocantes*.

THE ETIQUETTE OF GROCERIES

My Sundays in Paris constitute one giant cliché. I am woken by my neighbour's accordion music. He starts playing every Sunday morning at exactly half past nine and stops when he sits down with his wife and grandchildren to enjoy their weekly family lunch. Once dressed, I head out to the Rue des Martyrs, where a weekly ritual takes place. At this time, most tourists are still at their accommodation and the street is closed to cars. The entire street is filled with local residents doing their grocery shopping for Sunday lunch. Every time I walk here on Sunday morning, I find myself falling for the city all over again. There's no place where butchers are prouder of their sausages or where cakes and tarts look just so enticing. The same applies to the pretty shop windows, where tomatoes are displayed as if they were jewels, along with seasonal fruit on platters and entrecôtes decorated with roses.

This is the country where window dressers are actually considered artists and packaging designers are revered. Specialist shops often have their very own personalised wrapping paper, bags, boxes and packaging rituals. This is especially true on Rue des Martyrs.

This street inspired *New York Times* journalist Elaine Sciolino, who also lives nearby, to write her bestseller *The Only Street in Paris*. It describes the passion of Parisians for small entrepreneurs, the petition local residents started when one of the fish shops was forced to close its doors and the art of promenading and shopping that go hand in hand.

The latter is not to be underestimated. When I had just moved to Paris, I once made the capital mistake of storming into a chic boulangerie to buy a croissant after an early-morning run. Oh, the pitying looks... The average Parisian will dress decently even for something as trivial as picking up the mail.

BONJOUR MADAME

Another item of importance: greeting the personnel. While in many countries it's quite normal to enter a shop without greeting the staff present, in France this is inconceivable. And if you think a mere bonjour will do, you're mistaken. The phrase to use is *bonjour madame* or *bonjour monsieur*, preferably followed by *tout va bien?* It will be rewarded by a much better service. Another unwritten rule is that customers are to refrain from picking up items in specialty shops. There's a delicatessen around the corner from my house where they keep dried sausages on the counter. They look so delicious that it's hard to resist picking one up and going over to the register. I once made the mistake of doing this and barely managed to avoid being thrown out of the shop. Unfriendly? Not really: it has all to do with the love of sellers for their products. So don't confuse their pride with arrogance.

Lastly, it's very important not to be in any hurry. You can't really 'pop out' for some quick grocery shopping on a Sunday morning. Getting the job done properly will take you a few hours, but you'll return home with a bag full of treasures and a collection of beautiful wrappers. Next cliché: Sunday lunch. The accordion music has now been turned down and the courtyard of my apartment complex is full of the aromas of roasted chicken, stew and pies.

HAUTE LÉGUME

Should you have the idea that nothing else is eaten in Paris besides butter, oysters and sausages, you are very far from the truth. Fruit and vegetables play an essential role in Parisian gastronomy. Not just in restaurants, but at home as well. There are at least eight greengrocers within a 500-metre radius of my apartment, all of them veritable Gardens of Eden. Most are organic, others sell products from vendors located around Paris, such as my favourite Au Bout du Champs, which now has various shops around the city. They open late in the morning, because they pride themselves on the fact that everything they sell has been harvested just a few hours before. *Du champ à votre assiette en moins de 12h!* (From field to plate in less than 12 hours!) True-blue snobs order *les paniers d'Alain*: vegetables from the garden of three-star chef Alain Passard. In Paris these are delivered to your home.

The choice of fruit and vegetables is determined by the season. You should know that in France you don't have just the usual four seasons, but instead there are up to about eight hundred. There's fig season, cherry season, raspberry season and a season for horse lettuce. To talk about the mushroom season is selling it a bit short: there is the season for chanterelles, girolles (golden chanterelles), truffles and ceps. And let's not forget the season of the Coco de Paimpol, an AOC classified white bean. Should we ever make the mistake of forgetting, the chef of the Élysée Palace will certainly and kindly remind us on Instagram. Parisians go all in with their seasons. During fig season, the greengrocers have all varieties of fig on display. Pastry chefs prepare their fig tarts, cheese is served with preserved figs and chefs prepare their dishes with fig oil. As soon as the chestnut season starts, chestnuts are roasted in the streets, bakeries prepare their chestnut breads and menus include desserts with chestnut.

There's an ongoing competition to get *les primeurs*: the first vegetables of the season. This is a really old tradition, and even Louis XIV wanted to have the very first and freshest vegetable of the season. He ordered his horticulturist to think of a way to harvest asparagus in January, strawberries in March and peas in April. The horticulturist managed to satisfy Louis by building greenhouses and applying some smart tricks. This led him to be raised to the peerage.

HARICOTS VERTS

The great diversity in vegetables and fruit available in Paris aside, some things can be obtained everywhere at all times. One example is haricots verts, which the French eat all year round, both out and at home. Word has it that this bean was at the cradle of the *nouvelle cuisine*. Famous restaurant critics Henri Gault and Christian Millau were enjoying an extensive lunch at Paul Bocuse. When they returned that same evening for a meal, they asked the chef to prepare some light dishes for them. Bocuse made a salad with crisp haricots verts, followed by red mullet. The critics were moved by the simplicity on their plates, and voilà: a new and lighter cuisine was born. Bocuse himself was not at all impressed and stuck to the classic French cuisine. Even so, his salad has become a classic. When you are preparing Bocuse's salad yourself, be sure to use smaller haricots verts. The following applies to most vegetables: the tinier, the tastier.

HARICOTS VERTS SALAD

———— SERVES 4

500 grams of fresh haricots verts, preferably freshly harvested and small
1 large champignon de Paris or 2 small organic mushrooms
1 shallot
1 generous tablespoon of Dijon mustard
1 generous tablespoon of white wine vinegar
3 tablespoons of rapeseed oil, sunflower oil or peanut oil
Pepper & salt

———— PREPARATION ————

Cook the beans for 7 minutes in boiling water with some salt. Drain them and plunge into a bowl of cold water with some ice cubes to keep them fresh, green and crisp.

Chop the shallot very finely and the mushroom(s) into small pieces. Prepare the dressing. Stir together the mustard and vinegar and slowly pour in the oil. Keep stirring until you have a nice vinaigrette. Season with salt and pepper.

Mix together all the ingredients and leave to rest for a while. If you like, serve with a few slices of organic *foie gras* or duck breast.

GASTRONOMY FROM THE FREEZER

Not every Parisian has the opportunity to take time to do extensive shopping. This also immediately explains the success of the oddest shop I have ever set foot in: Picard. These supermarkets have everything – and when I say everything, I mean everything – you can imagine available in a frozen state, including the smile on the cashier's face. Picard is recognised by its clear blue logo with a white ice crystal. With over one thousand branches in France, most of them in Paris, you see their logo literally everywhere you look. Paris is actually where it all began in 1906 when Raymond Picard started his empire by delivering ice blocks used for cooling food.

Picard passed away a long time ago, but his company is still very much alive – and gigantic. Imagine the freezer aisle of your favourite supermarket, times fifty. Although it's not cold inside, it's not very cheerful either. As soon as they enter, customers immediately realise they are now in the frozen state of the Land of Cockaigne. From crêpes to croissants, sushi to éclairs and beurre blanc to cheese puffs, profiteroles and lemon cakes, mashed potatoes and escargots: these are all available here.

This awkward venue is really perfect for Parisians in a rush who don't have time for endless shopping during the weekend, but want their *pain au chocolat* for breakfast, macarons with their tea or *confit de canard* with pan-fried potatoes for dinner. At Picard, nothing is easier.

So although most chefs roll their eyes when the word Picard is uttered, almost everyone in Paris keeps something from them in their freezer. I love their resealable boxes of frozen chopped herbs, as I always have tarragon available when I need it. A great favourite among French people is their chocolate dessert *moelleux au chocolat*, of which one is sold by Picard every six seconds. The frozen croissants and puff pastry are another huge hit. But the most successful product in Paris ever is – you might have guessed – the haricots verts.

1200

CHEESES

Charles de Gaulle once wondered: how on earth do you govern a country that produces 246 varieties of cheese? He was right, and even today it is still a considerable challenge. In addition to being inextricably linked to strikes, demonstrations and protests, France is irrevocably connected with its cheeses. The average French person consumes half a kilo of cheese a week, and Paris is dotted with *fromageries* and *crémeries*, so you don't need to travel far for really good cheese. Around my apartment alone there are seven excellent cheese shops. I get my Corsican sheep cheese from one, Comté from another and camembert at the third. I buy new goat's cheese at the Friday afternoon market at Place d'Anvers. In addition, I always get at least one cheese I've never had before, hoping that one day I'll have tasted them all. This is quite the challenge. Those 246 cheese varieties Charles de Gaulle once mentioned? That number has since increased to over twelve hundred. Poor Macron…

AFFINEURS

The top-notch fromagers of Paris have ripening rooms where cheeses are allowed to develop their flavour. This ripening is considered an art, because a cheese will only come to life if perfectly matured, while the exact periods of time required for maturing are unknown. In addition, each cheese comes with its very own requirements: some are turned daily, others are brushed weekly and there are some that need to be drenched in wine. Some cheeses are ready in a few days, while others take two years to mature. And they are only good enough to be sold if their flavour is perfect.

Indicate at the fromagerie when you intend to consume your cheese. If it's for the next day, they'll give you perfectly mature cheese. If you plan on waiting a week before eating them, you'll have a somewhat less mature variant. One important tip: never buy too much. Parisians would rather serve one good cheese instead of an entire platter. If you want to serve an assorted selection of cheese, be sure to choose an uneven number. A common thread and difference in textures is also required. A goat cheese platter, for instance, is fine, but make sure it features hard and soft varieties. And then: select your bread with care. In Paris, cheese platters are generally served with some baguette or pain de campagne, but purists base their choice of bread on the cheese variety: pain de campagne to go with Saint-Nectaire, toasted bread with Mont-d'Or, wholewheat bread with Emmenthal and Comté. Crackers are hardly ever served with cheese, because the French consider them too dry.

CHEESE WAR

Quarrelling about food is daily business in France, but did you know that wars have actually been fought over it? There was the cheese war between France and Switzerland, which lasted for over ten years. And it was all because of Gruyère. Both countries make their own version of this cheese; the French version comes with holes, the Swiss without. The flavour also differs. Twenty years ago, Swiss Gruyère was awarded an AOC certification which protects the origin of products. Naturally, the French also wanted this prestigious certification for their Gruyère, to the fury of Swiss cheese makers. This resulted in a radical conflict. After a long and bitter legal battle, the French conceded – a painful defeat. Although French cheese makers can still produce cheese under the name of Gruyère, only the Swiss Gruyère is permitted to be sold and promoted under AOC.

And the French chefs? They use Swiss Gruyère more often than you'd imagine. It's also available from virtually every cheesemaker. After all: from cheese puffs to go with aperitifs to the onion soup by brasserie Au Pied de Cochon: without Swiss Gruyère, there would be no French cuisine.

♀ THREE FAVOURITES

Marie-Anne Cantin Daughter of a famous cheese affineur. She supplies top chefs and the Élysée Palace. *12 Rue du Champs de Mars, 7th*
Chez Virginie This tiny shop sells cheeses that are really hard to come by. Their goat cheese is particularly good. *54 Rue Damrémont, 18th*
Laurent Dubois This cheesemaker sells brie matured in Parisian cellars. His homemade butter is highly recommended. *97 Rue Saint Antoine, 4th*

RECIPE

GOUGÈRES

In France, these airy cheese choux buns are often served during aperitif or as an *amuse-bouche*. They're extremely easy to make and the dough is ready within five minutes. I use a recipe by top chef Alain Ducasse, who prepared his gougères using AOC Gruyère.

SERVES 4

100 ml of full-cream milk
100 ml of water
100 grams of salted butter, in pieces
Salt and optionally some pepper

100 grams of flour
125 grams of AOC Gruyère, grated
3 eggs, beaten

PREPARATION

Preheat the oven to 175 °C. Line a baking tray with baking paper.

In a pan with a thick bottom, bring the milk, water, butter, salt and pepper if desired to the boil. Add the flour and stir with a wooden spoon until the dough comes loose from the pan like a ball. This will take about a minute. Remove the pan from the heat and allow the dough to cool off.

Stir the eggs into the dough. Add 100 grams of the Gruyère and stir well.

Fill a piping bag with the dough and pipe balls on the lined baking tray. If you don't have a piping bag, use two spoons to make the balls. Space them out because they will rise and expand. Sprinkle them with the rest of the cheese. Bake them for 20 to 25 minutes until golden brown.

CHEESE ETIQUETTE

- French author Brillat-Savarin once said: a meal without cheese equals a beautiful woman with one eye. It goes to show that you cannot do without cheese after dinner.

- Cheese is an indispensable part of the French menu. It's never eaten as a snack, but instead as a course between the main dish and sweet dessert.

- Start with the cheese that has the softest flavour. Then eat cheeses clockwise and conclude with the cheese that has the strongest taste. Simply apply this rule of thumb: start with the cheeses with a white mould rind, continue with the red-moulded ones and save the blue-moulds for last.

- Strict rules apply for cutting cheese. Never cut the pointed end off a brie, because it holds most of its flavour. The correct way is to cut slices from the side. Round cheeses are cut in wedges. Parallel slices are cut from cylinder-shaped cheeses. The following applies to rectangular cheeses such as Comté: cut pencil-thick slices parallel to the crust.

- Never spread soft cheese on bread. It's not peanut butter. Another don't: holding a piece of cheese on your fork. Use a knife and pick up the cheese using a piece of bread.

- Take cheese from the fridge at least three hours before dinner.

- Don't take too much of a sweet with cheese. Compotes hardly ever add flavour, so walnuts, pecans, a few grapes or a pear are all better.

TOUT CARAMEL

When catering a dinner party at home, serving something sweet is almost mandatory. The same as before applies here: in Paris, it's normal not to prepare dessert yourself, but instead to buy a delicious ice cream cake or marvellous *baba au rum* from a good *glacier* or pastry chef. If you do want to prepare a homemade dessert, you could choose one of my three favourites: *île flottante* (floating island), tarte tatin or crème brûlée. Besides the fact that hardly anyone can resist them, they have another crucial thing in common: caramel. The French love it to the extent that it forms the base for most French confectionery.

The *île flottante* is the lightest and airiest of the three. Its islands of meringue float in creamy crème anglaise and are covered with caramel sauce. It's the perfect dessert after a lavish dinner. Even when you think you really couldn't swallow one more bite, you'll spoon up an *île flottante* without any trouble.

Tarte tatin – the apple pie that was accidentally invented by the Tatin sisters – is much richer. Instead of lining a baking mould with dough, the apples are put in first. After they are caramelised, the dough is put on top. Once baked, the tart is turned upside down. I eat it warm from the oven, preferably with some crème fraîche. Delicious, but also rather filling.

The perfect compromise is crème brûlée. Not just because it's everyone's best friend; it's also easy to prepare beforehand. All you have to do before serving is caramelise the layer of sugar on top of it, leaving you with all the time in the world to spend with your guests. And that's exactly what it's all about, in Paris in particular.

CRÈME BRÛLÉE XXL

A dessert doesn't come much more classic than a crème brûlée. I prepare mine based on a recipe by Bocuse, but generally as an XXL version so everyone can eat from the same dish. So instead of various small containers, choose one large one. Be sure to buy the good stuff in terms of ingredients: crème brûlée isn't half as good without exceptional cream and real vanilla.

SERVES 6-8

1 litre of double cream
2 vanilla pods
10 egg yolks (organic)

200 grams of granulated sugar
80 grams of cane sugar

PREPARATION

Preheat the oven to 150 °C. Add the double cream to a pan, split the vanilla pods lengthwise and add them to the cream. Turn off the heat as soon as the cream boils and set aside for 30 minutes. Meanwhile, whisk the egg yolks with the granulated sugar.

Remove the vanilla pods from the cream, scrape the remaining seeds from them and add to the cream. Add the lukewarm cream to the egg yolks and mix well.

Pour the mixture into a low and flat oven dish and bake for 50-60 minutes or until a thick custard is formed. Allow to cool and leave it in a cool place. Make sure the crème is cold before continuing. This means you can easily prepare it a day before eating it.

Sprinkle it with cane sugar and caramelise with a kitchen blow torch. If you haven't got a kitchen blow torch, simply put in under a hot grill for a few minutes.

À BIENTÔT

After all those years of shuttling between Amsterdam and Paris, you'd think I no longer need any suitcases. And although I've had two wardrobes, two china cabinets and two bookcases for quite some time now, I bring a giant suitcase every time I travel from Paris to Amsterdam. It's not filled with clothing but with food. So if ever we happen to meet on the train, please help me get my suitcase in the rack, because all those cans of *confit de canard* weigh more than you'd think. If you'd like to bring some Parisian souvenirs home, I have some tips for you.

SEVEN ITEMS TO BRING HOME FROM PARIS

- Cans of *confit de canard*. I usually buy the Dupérier variety, available at G. Detou. This is a splendid address for grocery shopping anyway. *58 Rue Tiquetonne, 2nd*

- I kid you not: canned patisserie is an actual thing here. The *gâteau de voyage* by Sébastien Gaudard is especially prepared to travel with you and has a long shelf life. I like the variety with lemon best. *22 Rue des Martyrs, 9th*

- If – like me – you are a *citron pressé* addict, be sure to bring a bottle of lemon juice by Pulco, available at supermarkets. This highly aromatic juice is turned into this delicious drink in no time at all.

- As much Alain Ducasse chocolate as possible. *40 Rue de la Roquette, 11th*

- A few pots of jam. Confiture Parisienne invents interesting flavour combinations such as champagne with strawberry or raspberry and pear. Jams by Christine Ferber are also excellent, and every variety you can possibly think of is available at Lafayette Maison's cellar. *35 Boulevard Haussmann, 9th*

- Various types of vinegar. There was a time when the French thought vinegar was a cure for the plague. It still has a vast array of uses, which is why many supermarkets sell a wide and wonderful selection.

- Wine! To bring home or enjoy during your train journey. Le Vin au Vert – a natural wine shop within walking distance of Gare du Nord – sells really good ones. *70 Rue de Dunkerque, 9th*

LES ADRESSES

Following are some of my favourites. Would you like to be informed of newcomers?

- I share new addresses on Instagram: @maragrimm
- These are also worth following: @parisismykitchen, @monpaname, @davidlebovitz, @parisbymouth

1st ARRONDISSEMENT

Astier de Villatte Ceramics by Astier de Villatte is made from clay retrieved from the bottom of the river Seine. *173 Rue Saint-Honoré*

À l'Épi d'Or A magnificent bistro owned by top chef François Piège. When you go there, you really should try their *steak haché*. *25 Rue Jean-Jacques Rousseau*

Café Isaka They sell delicious ice cream with Asian flavours, such as ube, pandan and sesame. *9 Rue Thérèse*

E. Dehillerin This world-famous kitchen shop sells copper pans of all types and sizes. *18 Rue Coquillière*

Hotel Costes For years and years, this roofed courtyard has been all about seeing and being seen. *7 Rue de Castiglione*

Boutique Yam'Tcha The very best teas and baos are sold here at the boutique of restaurant Yam'Tcha. *4 Rue Sauval*

Au Pied de Cochon This brasserie is open 24 hours a day; perfect if you get a sudden craving for oysters in the middle of the night. *6 Rue Coquillière*

Kei Chef Kei Kobayashi is the first Japanese chef in France to be awarded a third Michelin star. *5 Rue Coq Héron*

Sanjo Parisian summers are now inextricably linked to cold shio ramen by Sanjo. *29 Rue d'Argenteuil*

2nd ARRONDISSEMENT

19 Saint Roch The pure dishes with crunchy fresh vegetables by Pierre Touitou are absolutely worth trying – ask whether you can sit by the kitchen. *19 Rue Saint Roch*

Aux Lyonnais One of the oldest bistros in Paris. They serve classics such as *œufs en meurrette* and *pain perdu*. *32 Rue Saint-Marc*

Épices Roellinger This Mecca of spices sells dozens of pepper varieties. *51 Rue Sainte-Anne*

Cédric Grolet The Instagram-perfect cakes and croissants by Grolet are world-famous. *35 Avenue de l'Opéra*

G. Detou *Confit de canard*, mustard, *foie gras*… there's no end to what they sell here. *58 Rue Tiquetonne*

Le Petit Vendôme An old-school bistro that also serves *jambon-beurre*. *8 Rue des Capucines*

3rd ARRONDISSEMENT

Bing Sutt Inspired by a Hong Kong coffee bar. At lunchtime they serve a grand *char siu*. *22 Rue Béranger*

Jacques Genin If you'd like to enjoy cake and tart by my hero Genin, be at the doorstep first thing on Saturday morning or it'll be sold out. *33 Rue de Turenne*

Les Enfants du Marché Wine flows in abundance in this eatery at the Marché des Enfants Rouges. *39 Rue de Bretagne*

Chez l'Ami Louis One of the places to go for *foie gras*, escargots and other classics. *32 Rue du Vertbois*

Merci This department store is one of my favourites for table linen. *111 Boulevard Beau-marchais*

Caractère de Cochon A mini shop that sells very good charcuterie and the perfect *jambon-beurre*. *42 Rue Charlot*

Ogata Enjoy an extensive meal or sample tea varieties in this Japanese oasis. *16 Rue Debelleyme*

Le Mary Celeste A perfect address for cocktail fanciers. *1 Rue Commines*

4th to 6th ARRONDISSEMENTS

A.T. Atsushi Tanaka learned the trade from Pierre Gagnaire and runs an extremely fresh and precise kitchen. *4 Rue du Cardinal-Lemoine, 5ᵗʰ*

La Rotonde Not as well-known as other brasseries, but certainly just as good. *105 Boulevard du Montparnasse, 6ᵗʰ*

Kodawari A classic venue for *ramen*. *29 Rue Mazarine, 6ᵗʰ*

Poilâne One of the best bakeries in the city. *8 Rue du Cherche Midi, 6ᵗʰ*

Chez Marcel Flamboyant Pierre Cheucle welcomes guests to his charming bistro as if they were his prodigal children. *7 Rue Stanislas, 6ᵗʰ*

Lipp One of the few brasseries that is highly popular among Parisians, despite its mediocre quality. *151 Boulevard Saint-Germain, 6ᵗʰ*

Takuto In this hand roll bar owned by chef Takuya, guests enjoy excellent fish at the counter. *71 Rue de Seine, 6ᵗʰ*

Yen Once frequented by fashion legend Jane Birkin. Today, it's where her daughter Lou Douillon occasionally enjoys her book and a bowl of soba. *22 Rue Saint Benoît, 6ᵗʰ*

7ᵗʰ to 8ᵗʰ ARRONDISSEMENTS

Lastre Sans Apostrophe The smallest and best caterer in Paris. Be sure to taste their *pâté en croute*. *188 Rue de Grenelle, 7ᵗʰ*

Au Sauvignon I have been eating the same lunch here for years: a plate of smoked salmon with toasted Poilâne bread and a glass of wine. *80 Rue Saint-Pères, 7ᵗʰ*

Tapisserie A good address for breakfast and pastries – in particular their tart with maple syrup. *16 Avenue de la Motte Picquet, 7ᵗʰ*

La Grande Épicerie de Paris Dozens of different varieties of butter, shelves filled with vinegars and even more jams. I can spend hours here. *38 Rue de Sèvres, 7ᵗʰ*

Barthélémy From the façade to their packaging: everything about this cheese shop is a dream. *51 Rue de Grenelle, 7ᵗʰ*

Librairie Gourmande The city's cookery book heaven. *50 Rue Vavin, 7ᵗʰ*

9ᵗʰ ARRONDISSEMENT

Abri Soba This place is all about noodles, sake and natural wine. I love to come here because it's perfect for a quick lunch. *10 Rue Saulnier*

Bouillon Pigalle My favourite low budget address. Their *œufs mayo* and *babas au rum* are highly recommended. *22 Boulevard de Clichy*

Le Bon Georges A bistro in the higher price range with a classic but very good wine list and ditto *steak tartare*. *45 Rue Saint-Georges*

Hotel Amour When I didn't have my own place in Paris, I would often sleep here. I still come for the last orders. *8 Rue de Navarin*

Cuisine In this neo-bistro, Takao Inazawa combines the best of Asian and French cuisine. *50 Rue Condorcet*

Lafayette Maison If you don't have time to scour all chocolatiers in the city, you will find different ones on the ground floor of Lafayette Maison. Go to the cellar for the delicatessen. *35 Boulevard Haussman*

Union Boulangerie Good bread, even better croissants. *2 Rue Bleue*

Bouillon Chartier The oldest bouillon in the city. Their food may not be all that, but their ambiance certainly is. Do buy some of their iconic tableware on your way out. *7 Rue du Faubourg Montmartre*

Mamiche This is where I go for baguettes and almond croissants. *45 Rue Condorcet*

Torkia A few square metres of Tunisian street food heaven. The brunch served at their outdoor café is delicious. *79 Rue Blanche*

T'Xuan I really have a weak spot for this tearoom packed with chic Chinese Parisian women. *6 Rue La Fayette*

10th ARRONDISSEMENT

Les Arlots Of all restaurants in the city, this is where I like to eat the most. From their homemade terrine to the saucisse purée: nobody prepares it better than Thomas Brachet. *136 Rue du Faubourg-Poissonnière*

Billili It's always lively at this natural wine bar – and it has a good wine list. *136 Rue du Faubourg Poissonnière*

Terminus Nord One of those wonderful clichés: ordering oysters at this brasserie across from Gare du Nord just before you hop on your train. *23 Rue de Dunkerque*

Café les Deux Gares A neo-bistro perfect for an extensive lunch, quick coffee or a few drinks any time of the day. *1 Rue des Deux Gares*

Ten Belles Tiny little coffee and bread paradise. *10 Rue de la Grange aux Belles*

11th ARRONDISSEMENT

Folderol This is where the entire neighbourhood assembles for the improbable and fantastic combination of wine and ice cream. *10 Rue du Grand Prieuré*

Le Rigmarole Focus here is on yakitori and handmade pastas. And yes, this is a magnificent choice. *10 Rue du Grand Prieuré*

Kubri Shells with tahina; enjoy them at this Lebanese venue. *108 rue Amelot*

Café du Coin Open all day and always packed because of their popular natural wines and simple dishes. *9 Rue Camille Desmouilins*

Magma I am so very fond of the blend of the French and Japanese cuisine, particularly that of Ryuya Ono. *9 Rue Jean-Pierre Timbaud*

Double Dragon This is the home of French and Filipino fusion cuisine. You're not ready to leave until you have tried their bao with Comté and kimchi. *52 Rue Saint-Maur*

Reyna The coolest female chef in Paris is without question Erica Paredes. She gives a modern interpretation of Filipino cuisine. *41 Rue de Montreuil*

Oobatz Why you should eat pizza in Paris? Easy: because the sourdough made by Dan Pear is the best you'll ever have. *4 Avenue Jean Aicard*

Clamato Good address for *fruits de mer*. You can't book a table here, so be on their doorstep at 6:55 pm sharp. *80 Rue de Charonne*

Le Servan This neo-bistro with Asian influences is a perfect place to enjoy lunch. Nice little detail: they open on Mondays. *32 Rue Saint-Maur*

Septime The relaxed ambiance could almost make you forget that you are at one of the best (vegetable) restaurants in the world. *80 Rue de Charonne*

Jip This Korean eatery owned by Esu Lee is as cool as it gets. *112 Rue de la Roquette*

Chez Aline An all-time lively sandwich shop in a former butchers' shop. *85 Rue de la Roquette*

Bistrot Paul Bert A classic venue for *steak-frites*. *18 Rue Paul-Bert*

Mokonuts Lovely venue for a light lunch or good breakfast with Japanese and Lebanese influences. *5 Rue Saint-Bernard*

Maison Sota Sota Atsumi is one of the new generation of Japanese chefs who manage to take French gastronomy to a higher plane. *3 Saint Hubert*

La Buvette Teeny-tiny wine bar in a former cheese shop. *67 Rue Saint-Maur*

The Hood Asian street food is served here all day. *80 Rue Jean-Pierre Timbaud*

12th to 15th ARRONDISSEMENTS

Le Baron Rouge In this lively café, wine is served in the morning. They have oysters at weekends. *1 Rue Théophile Roussel, 12th*

Table Top restaurant owned by Bruno Verjus. Book a table at the bar from where you can see the kitchen. Do try their chocolate cake with caviar. *3 Rue de Prague, 14th*

Mosuke Chef Mory Sacko is known for is curious blend of African and French cuisine. *11 Rue Raymond-Losserand, 14th*

17th to 20th ARRONDISSEMENTS

L'Arpaon An unassuming neighbourhood bistro. Chef Yann Botbol previously worked at one of my great Parisian favourites: Le Servan. *57 Rue Montcalm, 18th*

Etsi This Greek neo-bistro is located in one of the nicest parts of Montmartre. They serve great Sunday lunches. *23 Rue Eugène Carrière, 18th*

Ama Siam I love this young version of the famous Lao restaurant Lao Siam. *49, Rue de Belleville, 19th*

Profil Grec This is the place for the very best Greek products. Many Parisian top chefs buy their olive oil here. I am addicted to their creamy feta. *109 Rue de Belleville, 19th*

Le Baratin A good address if you like offal. Their sweetbreads are particularly good. *3 Rue Jouye-Rouve, 19th*

Cheval d'Or This is where you'll find the best of Chinese and French fusion cuisine. *21 Rue de la Villette, 19th*

Bang Bang In this colourful establishment they serve – in their own words – banging hot food. Ah, don't worry: it's perfectly prepared and not too spicy. *9 Rue du Liban, 20th*

Dandelion Very good neo-bistro owned by chef Antoine Villard (formerly Septime). *46 Rue des Vignoles, 20th*

Copyright of the English edition
© Prestel Verlag, Munich · London · New York, 2026
A member of Penguin Random House Verlagsgruppe GmbH
Neumarkter Strasse 28 · 81673 Munich

1st edition 2026

produktsicherheit@penguinrandomhouse.de
(The above information is mandatory according to GPSR and should be used for all queries relating to the safety of our books.)

The publisher expressly reserves the right to exploit the copyrighted content of this work for the purposes of text and data mining in accordance with Section 44b of the German Copyright Act (UrhG), based on the European Digital Single Market Directive. Any unauthorized use is an infringement of copyright and is hereby prohibited.

Library of Congress Control Number is available; a CIP catalogue record for this book is available from the British Library.

First published in Dutch under the title *Bon Appétit Paris. Een culinaire Stijlgids vol Verhalen, Tips & Adressen uit Parijs* by Uitgeverij Grimm, Amsterdam
© Mara Grimm, 2022
www.maragrimm.nl

Photo credits: All photos by Arno Bosma and Mara Grimm, except:
p. 133 (bottom right): Copyright Fruttini; p. 196 (bottom): F. Flohic;
p. 40 (right) and p. 84 (right): Alamy Stock Photo.

Project management: Julie Kiefer
Texts: Mara Grimm
Photography: Arno Bosma & Mara Grimm
Art direction: Tara van Munster
Picture editor: Maaike Koorman
Cover illustration: Liv Lee van den Berg
Translation from Dutch: Gerrie Roorda for booklab, Munich
Copyediting: booklab, Munich
Typesetting: booklab, Munich
Production management: Luisa Klose
Printing and binding: Livonia Print, Riga

Penguin Random House Verlagsgruppe FSC®N001967
Printed in Latvia

ISBN 978-3-7913-9191-5
www.prestel.com